The Immigration Crisis

By Meghan Green

Cavendish
Square

New York

Published in 2021 by Cavendish Square Publishing, LLC
243 5th Avenue, Suite 136, New York, NY 10016

Website: cavendishsq.com

This publication represents the opinions and views of the author based on his or her personal experience, knowledge, and research. The information in this book serves as a general guide only. The author and publisher have used their best efforts in preparing this book and disclaim liability rising directly or indirectly from the use and application of this book.

Portions of this work were originally authored by Richard Brownell and published as *Immigration* (*Hot Topics*). All new material this edition authored by Meghan Green.

All websites were available and accurate when this book was sent to press.

Cataloging-in-Publication Data

Names: Green, Meghan.
Title: The immigration crisis / Meghan Green.
Description: New York : Cavendish Square, 2021. | Series: Topics today | Includes index.
Identifiers: ISBN 9781502657534 (pbk.) | ISBN 9781502657541 (library bound) | ISBN 9781502657558 (ebook)
Subjects: LCSH: Emigration and immigration law–United States–Juvenile literature. | Illegal aliens–United States–Juvenile literature. | Immigrants–United States–Juvenile literature. | United States–Emigration and immigration–Juvenile literature.| United States–Emigration and immigration–Government policy–Juvenile literature.
Classification: LCC KF4819.85 G73 2021 | DDC 325.73–dc23

Editor: Jennifer Lombardo
Copy Editor: Michelle Denton
Designer: Deanna Paternostro

Some of the images in this book illustrate individuals who are models. The depictions do not imply actual situations or events.

CPSIA compliance information: Batch #CS20CSQ: For further information contact Cavendish Square Publishing LLC, New York, New York, at 1-877-980-4450.

Printed in the United States of America

Find us on

CONTENTS

A CONTROVERSIAL SUBJECT

The United States has always been diverse; Native Americans are the only people living in the country who didn't have to travel to get to there or who didn't descend from these travelers. Some of these travelers were brought against their will as slaves. Many of the new inhabitants came specifically to take over the "New World." After the United States became its own country and a new government was established, people came as immigrants—not to take over the country, but to join it and become part of American society.

Throughout history, immigrants have been bullied and excluded. However, a new focus was placed on immigration during the 2016 US presidential election campaign, particularly in the case of people coming from Mexico. As of 2017, of the 44.5 million immigrants in the United States, approximately 10.5 million were here illegally, meaning they crossed the border unauthorized or chose to stay after their temporary visas expired. Of those undocumented immigrants, nearly 5 million were Mexican.

Immigration impacts how the nation conducts business, how it governs, and how citizens see themselves as individuals and as a society. There are differing opinions as to how the country should move forward with immigrants in mind.

For decades, the Statue of Liberty has been a beacon of hope for immigrants. However, the reality of life in the United States hasn't always matched up with immigrants' dreams.

Protests and New Policies

In 2007, immigrants and their supporters gathered across the country to protest proposals going through Congress that would crack down on illegal immigration. Many of the marchers were workers in service industry jobs who had lived in the United States for years but who feared deportation because they were unauthorized, or undocumented, immigrants. "After working 22 years here, paying taxes, and being a good citizen, I think it's fair they give me residency," said Los Angeles, California, protester Manuel Hernandez, an unauthorized immigrant from Mexico who marched with his wife and two children. "It's not fair we don't have documents."[1]

Hernandez's story was one that was repeated by many of the 20,000 protesters in Los Angeles that day. In Chicago, Illinois, 150,000 took to the streets to protest the breakup of mixed-status families, or families made up of authorized and unauthorized immigrants that could be split up if federal authorities arrested and deported mothers or fathers who could not prove their documented residency status. A gathering of 5,000 in New York City called for an end to immigration raids that rounded up thousands of unauthorized immigrants, as did another of 450 in Washington, DC.

Organizers and participants wanted to demonstrate that undocumented workers are hardworking, law-abiding people worthy of citizenship, but several counter-demonstrators voiced opposition to granting citizenship to millions of unauthorized immigrants. Jerry Hearty of Coolidge, Arizona, was one counter-demonstrator who lost his union-wage job in a meatpacking plant in Nebraska many years before when the company started

Most immigrants come to the United States because they want to build a better life for themselves and become part of American society.

hiring immigrants at lower wages. He claimed, "Now, no American can work at a packinghouse anymore because it's all minimum wage, and it's all illegal aliens [immigrants]."[2] Others like Hearty do not blame the companies seeking cheap labor but instead blame immigrants, whom they believe should follow the legal process of becoming citizens.

Today, the concerns of both sides are almost the same, but feelings have been heightened by the presidential administration of Donald Trump. Trump promised to build a wall on the border between the United States and Mexico to stop illegal immigration. Some people supported this, while others opposed it on the grounds that it would hurt people without actually stopping most illegal immigration. In 2018, with the wall still unbuilt, the Trump administration started a policy of detaining immigrants at the border and separating children from their parents. This move was met with outrage by many Americans, so the policy was revised. However, as of 2020, immigrants are still being detained in internment camps at the border.

Trump's policies have gained international attention, but he's far from the first president to focus on immigration. The administration of Barack Obama converted warehouses near the border into the detainment facilities the Trump administration gained infamy for using. Obama earned the nickname "Deporter-in-Chief" because of the huge number of unauthorized immigrants he deported, especially during his second term as president. In 2014 alone, more than 414,000 people were deported. However, immigration also decreased for years before Obama took office as some immigrants voluntarily left the country and fewer chose to arrive due to the US economic recession.

Because of the absence of constructive solutions to the immigration problems in the country, those who believe undocumented immigrants are the cause of both economic and social destruction are calling for strict reforms that may ultimately do more harm than good. It's an undeniable fact that immigrants have shaped America since before it became a country, and the nation has seen the economic consequences of decreased immigration.

At stake is the future of immigration in the United States. America is often seen as a land of opportunity by people in other countries looking to improve their lives. To maintain this image, it will need to reconcile the conflict that exists between some people's fantasies of a "perfect" America and the reality of being an economically developed and diverse country in the 21st century.

A BRIEF HISTORY OF IMMIGRATION

The United States is often called "a country of immigrants" because immigrants and their descendants make up the majority of the population. Native Americans, who were the only inhabitants of the continent before the colonists arrived, now make up only 1.6 percent of the population. Although immigration is now common in almost every country in the world, most other countries' populations have a far lower percentage of immigrants. For example, in Malaysia, about 62 percent of the population is indigenous, or native. Even in Australia, where aboriginal groups suffered the same kind of colonization and mass genocide as the Native Americans, aboriginals still make up about 3.3 percent of the population.

The European settlers who colonized North America came to what they called the New World seeking wealth and freedom, much like the immigrants who come to the United States every year. However, they didn't fit today's definition of "immigrant"—"a person who comes to a country to take up permanent residence"[1]—since there was technically no country to take up residence in, and the colonists' presence in Native American territory was far more disruptive to life on this continent than that of modern immigrants. Unlike today's immigrants, colonists from Spain, France, England, and the

When Europeans started arriving in North America, they didn't conform to the Native American way of life; they completely changed it. Today, Native Americans are still fighting for rights and recognition.

Netherlands conquered the native people who lived there before them and began erasing their culture, replacing it with a recreation of European society—one that mainly benefited white Christian people. Since then, each new group of immigrants has left their mark on American culture, but none have so fundamentally changed it.

Founded on Ideals

As it declared itself an independent nation in 1776, the United States also established itself as a beacon of hope for the huddled masses around the world. As a country founded on the principle that all people are created equal and with the right to "Life, Liberty, and the pursuit of Happiness," as the Declaration of Independence states, it was primed from the beginning to become a destination for those who wanted a better life. Governed by a democratically elected legislature and president, America was truly a novelty in the 18th and 19th centuries, and it attracted those who were being oppressed by monarchies and dictatorships in their home countries. It also operated on a free market economy that allowed virtually anyone to go into business for themselves, and it seemed that the only limit to a person's success in America was how hard they were willing to work. Immigrants came to the United States expecting to be welcomed with open arms. The idealized notion was that their ethnicity, religion, and social status would be of little consequence after they became full citizens—Americans before anything else. Becoming a citizen, however, was no easy task.

To immigrate to the United States, people voyaged across thousands of miles of ocean from Europe and Asia, or crossed the barren desert region separating the United States from Central and South America. Leaving families that they often never saw again, immigrants sometimes came to this country with little or no knowledge of the English language or American customs. Although many new jobs were created as the Industrial Revolution came to America and the country spread westward, there was never enough work for everyone, and employers and landlords often took advantage of immigrants. Living conditions in the cities where most immigrants settled were crowded and unsanitary, which led to disease as well

This 1931 photo shows American immigration officials examining Japanese immigrants on their ship before allowing them into the United States.

as cultural conflict as people from vastly differing countries were forced to live in close proximity to each other. Outside their communities, they were faced with bigotry and hatred from native-born Americans who saw them as inferior.

Despite these hardships, immigrants continued to arrive in the United States in large numbers. The opportunity to make life better for themselves and their families was too good for people to be deterred by the stories they might have heard about the mistreatment of their fellow immigrants. To many, anything was possible in America, and the struggle was more than worth it.

Western European Immigrants

The small amount of immigration to the United States in the early years of the American republic was not well documented, and the best population estimates combined with passenger manifests of ships arriving in American ports place the yearly average at

6,000 people up until 1820. The US Census—a survey taken every 10 years to determine the number and makeup of people living in the United States—was first conducted in 1790, but it only counted the number of free men and women as well as the number of enslaved Africans. It didn't inquire about a person's nation of origin, and it was quite simplistic compared to the modern census, which includes questions about what kind of housing a person lives in, where they're from, whether they have a disability, their income, and more.

Turmoil in Europe as a result of the French Revolution of 1789 and the Napoleonic Wars that devastated Europe until 1814 significantly limited immigration. Many able-bodied men were drafted into the armies of the various warring nations, and Europe's war-ravaged economy left little money for private citizens to buy passage on a ship. A number of private shipping companies were pressed into military service or went out of business, so there was considerably less transatlantic travel. The War of 1812 between the United States and Great Britain also curtailed immigration because there's little motivation to immigrate to a nation in the middle of a war.

After this period of upheaval, a sustained period of prosperity in the United States led to enormous economic and territorial expansion, two factors that proved very inviting to would-be immigrants. More than 2.5 million immigrants came to America in a 30-year period beginning in 1820. This played an important role in the rapid growth of the population, which rose from 9.6 million that year to just over 23 million in 1850, one of the highest growth rates in the world and in history.

A vast majority of these immigrants came from Western Europe, with the bulk of them from Germany, Ireland, France, and Great Britain. The Irish were driven to America by widespread famine in their home country, while the rest of the European arrivals were mainly motivated by economic factors. Europe was rapidly industrializing during this time, and a large number of agricultural jobs disappeared as land and labor were lost to factories and commercial expansion. While the United States was also industrializing at an accelerated rate, there was far more land available for

The Irish Potato Famine had devastating consequences all across Ireland. Those who could afford to do so left the country because food was so scarce. Shown here is a depiction of a food riot in the city of Galway in Ireland during this time.

agricultural development. Additionally, the development of steamships and railroads further facilitated the ease of travel across Europe to the coast, where passage could be obtained to cross the Atlantic to America.

Beginning in 1850, the American population began to feel the effects of large-scale immigration. Until 1830, immigrants accounted for only 1.5 percent of the population. By 1850, when the US Census began recording place of birth, immigrants had risen to nearly 10 percent of the population. The California Gold Rush of 1849 brought the first significant wave of immigration from nations outside Europe, with immigrants arriving from China, Australia, Mexico, and South America. Additionally, the end of the Mexican-American War in 1848 resulted in the United States gaining a large amount of territory from Mexico, leading to the automatic US citizenship of about 75,000 Mexicans living in that region.

Southern and Eastern European Immigrants

While immigrants continued to arrive in a steady stream from Western Europe, the number who arrived from Southern and Eastern Europe began to rise sharply in the last decades of the 19th century.

Exploiting Irish Immigrants

Some 19th-century newspaper ads for female domestics, or maids, included the words, "No Irish need apply," although it may be an urban myth that this sentiment appeared on virtually every "Help Wanted" sign. As Richard Jensen of the University of Chicago argued, "Evidence from the job market shows no significant discrimination against the Irish—on the contrary, employers eagerly sought them out."[1]

However, the reason for their popularity may have been their willingness to do hazardous tasks for low wages. According to the Library of Congress,

Irish immigrants often entered the workforce at the bottom of the occupational ladder and took on the menial and dangerous jobs that were often avoided by other workers. Many Irish women became servants or domestic workers, while many Irish men labored in coal mines and built railroads and canals. Railroad construction was so dangerous that it was said, "[there was] an Irishman buried under every tie."

As Irish immigrants moved inland from eastern cities, they found themselves in heated competition for jobs ... This competition heightened class tensions and, at the turn of the century, Irish Americans were often antagonized by organizations such as the American Protective Association (APA) and the Ku Klux Klan.[2]

1. Richard J. Jensen, "'No Irish Need Apply': A Myth of Victimization," *Journal of Social History* 36, no. 2 (2002): p. 405.

2. "Irish—Joining the Workforce," Library of Congress, accessed February 28, 2020, www.loc.gov/teachers/classroommaterials/presentationsandactivities/presentations/immigration/alt/irish4.html.

The industrialization and resulting economic prosperity in Western Europe did not spread to the south and east, and immigrants from those areas fled the poor economic and social conditions with growing frequency. In 1870, the census reported 93,824 foreign-born persons from Eastern and Southern Europe, which accounted for 6 percent of all immigrants. By 1910, more than 4.5 million foreign-born persons from Eastern and Southern Europe were living in the United States, coming mainly from Poland, Russia, and Italy. By this point, nearly two-thirds of all immigrants came from Eastern and Southern Europe.

With the arrival of people from this region, the general makeup of European immigration to America began to change, and with it America's attitude toward immigrants. Most of the immigrants from Western Europe were light-skinned and Protestant, which was the predominant religious faith in the United States. The Irish, many of whom were Catholic, were a notable exception, and they faced numerous difficulties in the United States because of their faith. Groups of Protestant Americans, such as the Order of the Star-Spangled Banner and the Order of United Americans, heaped scorn and ridicule—and sometimes violence—upon Catholics from Ireland and other nations, mainly because they feared that the continued arrival of Catholic immigrants would threaten the Protestant majority in the United States. Irish Catholics in particular were sometimes turned away by private employers and ended up taking public-sector jobs in many cities as municipal workers.

Many of the immigrants from Eastern and Southern Europe also faced discrimination because their skin wasn't as fair, or light, which made them visibly different from the majority of the population. Jewish immigrants often remained within their own communities and rarely mixed with outsiders, which made many native-born Americans suspicious of them. Their religion was seen as strange by many citizens in the overwhelmingly Christian nation.

Jewish, Irish, and other immigrants from Europe often settled in urban areas that were predominantly poor and filthy. The conditions of these neighborhoods were a result of poor urban planning and a complete lack of municipal services, such as trash collection,

Many immigrants could only afford housing in overcrowded, dirty tenement slums such as these. However, as the washing hanging on the lines makes clear, myths about their lack of cleanliness were unfounded.

sewage treatment, and health codes—all things taken for granted today. However, the immigrants were blamed for the terrible conditions of the inner cities, which contributed to persistent myths about how immigrants were dirty and lazy.

In fact, immigrants were more often than not blamed for society's ills. In an 1896 article for *Atlantic Monthly*, economist Francis A. Walker implied that immigrants are universally poor, stupid, and violent, and he suggested that America should not expose itself to such people for fear of degrading its culture. Although these beliefs were based in ignorance, they were surprisingly popular then and are still used in arguments against immigration today.

Controlling Immigration

Immigration policy was left mainly to the states for the first 70 years of US history, but a series of Supreme Court decisions in 1849 known as the Passenger Cases began chipping away at state control. The federal government had grown angry at the collection of special taxes from immigrants by several states, and the court ruled that they didn't have the power to collect such taxes. Congress went further in 1864, passing legislation that took control of immigration policy from the states, and by 1875, the Supreme Court had effectively ruled that the establishment and regulation of immigration policy fell under the federal government's constitutional power to regulate interstate commerce. This was done in part to bring order to a system in which scattered state procedures over immigration often contradicted one another.

Once these Supreme Court precedents were established, the federal government stepped in to create a structured system to control immigration. The first federal act to deliberately set a standard was the Chinese Exclusion Act of 1882. This act rose out of complaints about Chinese immigrants, more than 300,000 of whom had settled in the West since the California Gold Rush, seeking to escape turbulent political conditions in China. Many found work as cheap labor on the railroads and as domestic servants in California and the western territories, where they were blamed for driving down wages. The Exclusion Act's passage barred Chinese immigration to the United States for a period of 10 years, and this 10-year period was renewed several times until the law was repealed in 1943.

In 1892, when the 9.2 million immigrants in the United States represented 15 percent of the population, the federal government took control of immigration at the Port of New York, establishing Ellis Island as the national reception center for people seeking entry into the United States. Everyone who came to Ellis Island and other ports of entry was subjected to literacy tests and health examinations. Those with tuberculosis or other contagious diseases were either turned back or forced to live in quarantine for extended periods of time. The literacy tests were an attempt to control the quality of immigrants who were let into the country. People were further evaluated for the labor skills they possessed, which allowed the government to keep an overabundance of workers with particular job skills from driving down wages for citizens.

In 1907, Senator William P. Dillingham established the US Immigration Commission. This body, historically known as the Dillingham Commission, investigated the occupations and living standards

THE AMERICANESE WALL, AS CONGRESSMAN
BURNETT WOULD BUILD IT.

UNCLE SAM: You're welcome in — if you can climb it!

As this political cartoon from the early 1900s shows, efforts to restrict
immigration—and resistance to those efforts—are not new concerns.

of immigrants in the United States and came to the biased and false conclusion that immigrants from Eastern and Southern Europe possessed a higher risk for criminal behavior, poverty, illness, and lower intelligence than immigrants who had come to America previously.

Based in part on the results of the Dillingham Commission, the federal government passed a series of strict immigration quotas to limit the number of new arrivals. The Emergency Quota Act of 1921 limited the number of immigrants from each nation to 3 percent of that nation's total population in the United States as reported in the 1910 Census. This act heavily favored immigration from Western Europe because immigrants had been coming from that region for much longer, resulting in higher populations in the United States. The National Origins Act of 1924 further restricted immigration from each country to 2 percent of that nation's total population in the United States in 1890. Together, these acts greatly reduced mass immigration in the United States for much of the rest of the 20th century.

A Steep Drop

Because of the passage of the two 1920s immigration laws, as well as the Great Depression in the 1930s, the number of immigrants steadily decreased. Between 1930 and 1940, the number of immigrants in the country dropped from 14.2 million to 11.5 million.

World War II continued to keep immigration low, but the federal government did allow several thousand Mexican laborers into the country to work in agricultural jobs. Known as the Bracero Program (*bracero* is the Spanish word for "worker"), this use of temporary labor offset the large number of jobs left open by the drafting of millions of male US citizens into the armed forces. Between 1942 and 1964, 4.6 million contracts were signed, although some people came back multiple times on different contracts.

After the Allied victory brought an end to World War II in 1945, the American economy grew tremendously, but immigration was still controlled by strict quotas. The McCarran-Walter Immigration Act of 1952 reaffirmed the national-origins quota system, allowing only 154,277 visas to be issued each year. Various refugee relief acts did allow individuals from war-torn countries in Europe and Asia into the United States in the late 1940s and early 1950s, although many people opposed these acts. Additionally, the War Brides Acts of 1945 and 1946 allowed foreign-born wives and fiancées of US servicemen to immigrate.

In 1954, the federal government carried out a mass deportation of thousands of undocumented immigrants from Mexico. It was estimated in the decade preceding this deportation that the number of undocumented immigrants had risen 6,000 percent, with 1 million coming in 1954 alone, taking advantage of the open border and high number of available jobs. The US Border Patrol, with the help of federal, state, and local authorities in Texas, Arizona, New Mexico, and California, returned many to Mexico. It remains unknown exactly how many returned to their native country of their own choice, or whether they remained in Mexico or simply crossed back into the United States after the sweep ended.

Because so many American men were fighting in World War II, the Bracero Program was essential to the United States. Mexican laborers kept farms working to provide food to the country. Shown here are braceros relaxing in their bunkhouse after a long day of work.

Into the 21st Century

In 1965, the US Congress passed the Immigration and Nationality Act, also known as the Hart-Celler Act, which effectively replaced many of the immigration quotas that had been in place for decades. An annual limit of 170,000 visas was established for immigrants from countries in the Eastern Hemisphere, with no more than 20,000 per country. Another cap of 120,000 immigrants from the Western Hemisphere was also put in place, with visas available on a first-come, first-serve basis. There was no cap placed on family reunification visas, which allowed immigrants who attained citizenship to sponsor the immigration of adult relatives.

After the passage of the Hart-Celler Act, immigration was once again on the rise. In the 1970s, 4.5 million people came to the United States, with Latinx making up 40 percent of the total. Another 5.6 million immigrants entered the country in the 1980s, and 11 million more came in the 1990s. These numbers include unauthorized immigrants; by 2015, about 11 percent of all immigrants were living in the country illegally.

The percentage of Latinx making up the foreign-born population rose dramatically from the 1980s until about 2009, but it stagnated for years and then started declining. In fact, 2017 marked the first year since the 1990s that Mexicans, in particular, made up less than half of all unauthorized immigrants. Although immigrants still come to the United States from Europe, their numbers are only a fraction of what they once were. They lost their majority status among foreign-born people in the United States in 1980, signifying the end of an era of American immigration. As a new era of immigration began, the United States could no longer look to the past to predict what effect the immigrants of the 21st century would have.

Your Opinion Matters!

1. How are colonists different than immigrants?
2. Do you agree or disagree with the immigration acts that were passed in the 1800s and 1900s?
3. Where did your family immigrate from originally?

NEW MILLENNIUM, NEW IMMIGRATION PATTERNS

Immigration history in the United States has set the stage for how immigrants are viewed and treated in the 21st century. The country has a somewhat contradictory history of both welcoming and scorning immigrants, and this holds true today.

Today, there are more than 44.5 million immigrants living in the United States, accounting for about 13.7 percent of the country's population. This is close to the historic high of 14.8 percent that was recorded in 1890. About 10.5 million of them are undocumented. Most immigrants, whether documented or undocumented, come from Mexico, China, and India, although every country on Earth is represented. Immigrants come to the United States now for the same reasons they have come throughout history: for better economic and social opportunities, and by extension, better lives. Since the Hart-Celler Act removed the quota system, immigration has boomed in America. The United States attracts newcomers like a magnet; its labor-hungry, capitalist economy is in constant need of new workers, especially ones who are willing to work for minimum wage. Even this image of immigrants, though, is changing.

◀ Many immigrants are excited to become Americans. They work hard to make that dream happen, and taking their citizenship oath, as this Indian family is doing, is a cause for celebration.

Misconceptions About Immigrants

Contrary to popular belief, almost half of all immigrants work white-collar jobs, and although many still work in fields such as agriculture, food service, and construction, a growing number of immigrants are getting jobs in information technology, life sciences, and high-tech manufacturing. Since 2010, the number of college-educated immigrants allowed into the country has jumped from 29 to 44 percent, and they are now overrepresented in most science, technology, engineering, and math (STEM) fields. The American economy, measured by its gross domestic product (GDP)—the total value of all goods and services produced within the nation's borders—was about $20 trillion in 2019, the largest in the world. That, in part, is due to the large number of skilled immigrants now making above-average income and paying higher taxes.

Despite all this, immigrants are often still treated poorly. Discrimination and racism play a daily part in many immigrants' lives, putting them in difficult and sometimes dangerous positions even if

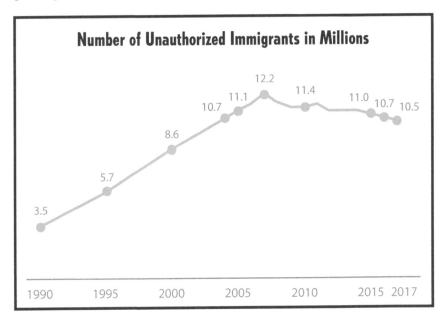

Number of Unauthorized Immigrants in Millions

3.5   5.7   8.6   10.7   11.1   12.2   11.4   11.0   10.7   10.5

1990   1995   2000   2005   2010   2015   2017

The number of unauthorized immigrants in the United States has generally been decreasing since 2007, as this information from the Pew Research Center shows.

they arrived in the country legally. This is especially true if they are a person of color or have difficulty speaking English. Even though it's illegal to do so, employers and landlords may deny applications from immigrants based on their name or style of dress. Hate groups such as the Ku Klux Klan (KKK) target them. In the case of unauthorized immigrants, they may be arrested and deported at any time and taken away from their families and friends. It has always been hard to be an immigrant in the United States, but as racial and political tensions rise, life for many immigrants in 21st-century America has become a harrowing experience.

Latinx Immigrants

The US Office of Management and Budget defines "Hispanic" or "Latinx" as "a person of Cuban, Mexican, Puerto Rican, South or Central American, or other Spanish culture or origin regardless of race."[1] Although Hispanic and Latinx are used interchangeably on the US Census, they're not the same. Hispanic refers to someone who speaks Spanish, while Latinx refers to someone from Latin America. Therefore, someone from Spain would be Hispanic but not Latinx, someone from Brazil would be Latinx but not Hispanic, someone from Mexico would be both, and someone from Portugal would be neither. Latinx were the fastest-growing ethnic group in the United States until 2013 and still represent the largest minority in the country as of 2020. However, they are expected to be surpassed by Asians by 2065.

As with most other immigrants, Latinx immigrants come to the United States mainly for economic reasons. Mexico, for example, has the second-largest economy in Latin America but is poorer than its northern neighbor, with a GDP of $1.3 trillion and a large gap between the rich and poor citizens. Despite recent economic growth, jobs in Mexico are scarce and pay little, and jobs in the United States in the farming, construction, and service industries are easier to come by. These occupations pay little compared to other jobs in the United States, but the salaries are frequently many times higher than what similar work would pay in Mexico.

This disparity, or difference, has led many in Mexico to move to

Seeking Asylum

"Asylum" describes political protection for certain immigrants who are fleeing danger in their home countries. While refugees are people who apply to live in the United States before they leave their home country, people seeking asylum do so afterward. They come to the country before getting the proper permission, but once officials determine that they meet the criteria for asylum, they can begin applying for refugee status. Seeking asylum in the United States is not and never has been illegal. However, the Trump administration has worked to roll back asylum protections, claiming that as many as 90 percent of immigrants abuse the system by making false claims. However, research has proven the administration's claims false. Generally, only about 20 to 30 percent of asylum claims are granted, but the remaining cases are often dismissed not because they're false, but due to improperly completed paperwork or confusion about the system, especially if a language barrier is involved. For instance, many immigrants assume their interview with an asylum officer counts as an application, unaware that they have to fill out a paper application. Other cases are closed because the individual is granted other benefits through a different court system and therefore no longer needs their asylum approved.

In June 2018, Jeff Sessions, who was the attorney general at the time, announced that the courts could deny asylum to victims of gang violence and domestic violence. After this announcement, many women who came to the United States to escape these kinds of violence were suddenly considered to have come to the country illegally. Instead of being helped, they were arrested and detained indefinitely or deported. Sessions received criticism for his decision from civil rights groups because he called domestic violence a "private crime," which, according to experts, is not a legal term. Some people, such as Mara Verheyden-Hilliard of the Partnership for Civil Justice Fund, accused Sessions of returning to the outdated belief that domestic violence is a private matter between a couple. This belief, Verheyden-Hilliard and others say, places thousands of women in danger both in and out of the United States.

the United States—often illegally—with the hope of finding better jobs. However, when the United States entered an economic recession in 2007, many Mexicans left the country. For the same reason, fewer Mexicans were entering the country. In 2017, Mexicans accounted for 47 percent of all unauthorized immigrants, compared to 57 percent a decade prior.

Undocumented immigrants of all races travel to wherever jobs can be found within the United States, but they have traditionally migrated to major metropolitan areas. Six states—California, Texas, Florida, New York, New Jersey, and Illinois—account for 57 percent of the unauthorized immigrant population.

Asian Immigrants

Since 2010, immigrants to the United States have been more likely to come from East or South Asia than from Latin America. In 2017, almost 40 percent of new arrivals were Asian, compared to about 27 percent Latinx. Asian Americans and Pacific Islanders now account for nearly 7 percent of the US population. Most come from India, China, the Philippines, Vietnam, and Korea on family-sponsored visas, joining family members who are already native-born or naturalized citizens.

Like Latinx immigrants, Asian immigrants come to the United States to build better lives for their families. However, unlike most Latinx immigrants, many Asian immigrants are coming to America to go to school before looking for work. According to a report by the Council of Graduate Studies, China, India, and South Korea lead international applications to American graduate schools. Because of the recent economic upturns in these countries, more and more young Asians can afford America's high tuition costs and are able to travel abroad to go to college. These young people then graduate and are recruited into high-skill fields, where they generally thrive.

Although Asian immigrants are generally better received than their Latinx counterparts, many continue to feel estranged from American culture. According to the Pew Research Center, when asked if they felt like "typical Americans," 53 percent said no, and when asked if they felt they had been personally discriminated

The general view of Asian immigrants tends to be that they are smart, successful, and wealthy. These "positive" stereotypes often mask racism toward them, making Americans believe it doesn't exist.

against in the past year, 19 percent said yes. Due to language and cultural barriers that can exist along with racism and cultural stereotypes, American society hasn't done well at reaching out to Asian immigrants despite taking them in for almost two centuries. Because of this, Asian immigrants are often segregated into "Chinatowns," "Little Tokyos," or "Little Indias," in much the same way that Latinx immigrants are, and the barriers are seldom broken down.

Impact on Cities

The growth of immigrant communities in the United States has led to a debate about the impact of mass immigration on America's urban centers. City dwellers across the United States consume vast amounts of water, food, electricity, and other items that must be carefully measured by urban planners to prevent shortages. Through the study of birth rates and the migration trends of the native-born population, planners can predict increasing and decreasing demand for a variety of systems necessary to successful urban management, such as water and sewage treatment, power supply, and transportation. However, it's difficult to meet the needs of cities with large immigrant communities because they grow faster than urban planners can account for and adapt to their needs.

The Federation for American Immigration Reform (FAIR), a national lobbying group that seeks improved border security and stricter controls on immigration, claims that these communities, which grow larger every year, are primarily responsible for urban sprawl, which is the unrestricted outward growth of cities that often harms the surrounding environment and puts a strain on natural resources. However, studies into this claim have shown that native-born Americans are more likely than immigrants to contribute to urban sprawl. Furthermore, FAIR has been classified as a hate group by the Southern Poverty Law Center (SPLC), a nonprofit organization that tracks and studies hate groups. The SPLC explained, "The bottom line is, FAIR doesn't peddle facts; it peddles hate. Its lobbying and legal efforts ... are based on fomenting [creating] fear, on exploiting racial tensions and economic anxieties to convince people that they had better not let any more 'aliens' into their country."[2]

Contrary to FAIR's claims, immigration to large metropolitan areas may actually be helping the United States. As major centers of trade and culture, cities such as New York and Los Angeles are highly likely to host immigrant entrepreneurs once they have learned English and become citizens. Ted Hesson from *The Atlantic* stated:

> ... there is ample evidence that immigrants are creating businesses and revitalizing the U.S. workforce. From 2006 to 2012, more than two-fifths of the start-up tech companies in Silicon Valley had at least one foreign-born founder, according to the Kauffman Foundation. A report by the Partnership for a New American Economy, which advocates for immigrants in the U.S. workforce, found that they accounted for 28 percent of all new small businesses in 2011.

Because of high population numbers, urban sprawl affects cities all over the world. Shown here is Manila—the capital of the Philippines—which is one of the most densely populated cities on Earth.

> … immigration, on the whole, bolsters the workforce and adds to the nation's overall economic activity. Look at the impact on cities that attract the most foreign-born residents. New York, Los Angeles, Chicago, and Houston are all major immigrant destinations and also economic powerhouses, accounting for roughly one-fifth of the country's gross domestic product. In New York, immigrants made up 44 percent of the city's workforce in 2011; in and around Los Angeles, they accounted for a third of the economic output in 2007. [3]

Therefore, for all that an increasing population may strain a nation's resources, immigrants tend to give back as much as they take.

Illegal Immigration

Experts estimate that there are about 10.5 million unauthorized immigrants in the United States—a decrease of 14 percent from 2007. Although unauthorized immigrants make up only about 3.2 percent of the US population as a whole, politicians often use the number "11 million" to scare people into thinking the country is being overrun, causing significant alarm among US lawmakers and citizens.

Unauthorized immigrants tend to fall into one of two categories: those who cross the border undocumented, and those who were admitted legally and have overstayed their visas. They are motivated to come to the United States for economic reasons, much like authorized immigrants, but there are additional factors that drive them to cross the border illegally or refuse to leave after their visas have expired. As the American Immigration Council pointed out, "Many people wonder why all immigrants do not just come to the United States legally or simply apply for citizenship while living here without authorization. These suggestions miss the point: There is no line available for unauthorized immigrants and the 'regular channels' are largely not available to prospective immigrants who end up entering the country through unauthorized channels."[4]

As of 2020, the only way a person can legally immigrate to the United States is if they already have a family member in the country, if they're offered a job, or if they're seeking asylum. Some people worry about the first reason causing a "chain migration," where people come over for work and then sponsor their family members. In these people's minds, chain migration is dangerous because it allows too many people into the country. However, this is a myth that's mainly based in xenophobia, or fear of foreigners. The laws in place regarding bringing immediate family members over are based on a 1965 law established to reunite families. *Politico Magazine*, run by the website Politico, explained:

> *Under this law, when you fall in love and marry that guy you met while working in Shanghai, our immigration law is set up so that you can bring him home. And his 2-year-old. And when your family grows and you'd like his parents to help with child care,*

while it takes quite a few years, you'd ultimately be able to bring them, too.

If we had a family immigration system without limits, this structure could theoretically lead to the dreaded chain migration. In addition to allowing you to bring that Chinese spouse, his child and ultimately his parents, once your spouse is a U.S. citizen, he can petition for his sister and her family. And in theory, once her spouse becomes a citizen, he could do the same for his siblings. But we don't have an unlimited system. In fact, back in 1988, the federal agency then known as the General Accounting Office found that the immigration system's waiting lists make chain migration a theory that doesn't really happen in practice.[5]

Some companies offer guest worker visas, which allow people such as this fruit picker to come into the United States for a short time to work legally. If they don't leave when their visa expires, they're considered an unauthorized immigrant.

Applying to live in the United States is a complicated process that can involve long waits of months or even years. Furthermore, the applications can be confusing and the process can be expensive. Some people can't afford to gather together all the documents they need, and having a language barrier can make it easy to make mistakes that cause their application to be rejected. Even people who do everything right can be rejected, and many are never told why. Many who wish to come to the United States to work would rather skip the bureaucracy, and those who are fleeing danger don't have time to wait and see if they're approved. Some don't intend to stay in America indefinitely, though many end up doing just that.

It's difficult to determine how many unauthorized immigrants there are in the United States, and estimates vary widely. The very nature of their undocumented status makes it difficult to locate and track them, and many do their best to maintain a low profile. In recent years, 11 million has been the number accepted by the media and the federal government. Some dispute this estimate, although there's little research to back up such contrary claims. The National Association of Former Border Patrol Officers (NAFBPO), for example, claims there are 18 to 20 million unauthorized immigrants, but this claim was made in an open letter by the NAFBPO chairman, not in an official study.

With the media and politicians pointing fingers at Mexico as the source of illegal immigration, it's important to remember that, although Mexicans make up nearly half of unauthorized immigrants, they are by no means the only ones in the country. Mexico, however, is unique in that it shares a border with the United States, making the United States the easiest country for Mexicans to get to, which is the simplest explanation as to why there's a disproportionate number of Mexicans in the unauthorized immigrant population. The Mexican-American border used to be very easy to cross, even though the journey was hazardous. To many people looking for work, the rewards outweighed the risks.

A Dangerous Journey

Although immigrants can be jailed and deported for be-

Citizenship on the Census

The US Census Bureau oversees two questionnaires. Originally, there was only one: the census, taken every 10 years. Most households would get a short version of the census to fill out, but one in six would get a longer version that asked more questions. In the early 2000s, this longer survey was replaced with a yearly survey called the American Community Survey (ACS). It's sent out on a rotating basis, so no family gets it more than once every five years.

In 2019, the Trump administration tried to have a question about citizenship status added to the 2020 census. The Supreme Court blocked this move as unconstitutional, and while Trump tried to fight the decision for a while, he eventually admitted defeat. Vox explained why many people disapproved of the question:

Trump backing off is a major victory for Democrats and activists who have challenged the move, and for people who simply want the census to be accurate. Including the question, experts warned, could have resulted in lower response rates among noncitizens and Latinos (which many believed was in fact the Trump administration's goal) ...

ing in the United States illegally, criminal enforcement of illegal immigration is a relatively recent phenomenon, arising mainly from concerns that unauthorized immigrants are putting a strain on government resources. Previously, the lack of immigration enforcement and poor security along the 2,000-mile (3,219-kilometer) southern border allowed millions to come into the United States illegally without fear of being caught. In addition, government agencies in charge of tracking expired visas couldn't handle the backlog that developed with large numbers of immigrants, allowing unauthorized immigrants to continue living in the United States.

Getting caught and returned to their native country, however, is only one of the dangers unauthorized Mexican immigrants face. Crossing the border can be extremely hazardous, particularly in the

> *The census is ideally supposed to count every person residing in the United States—citizens, noncitizen legal residents, and unauthorized residents. The state results are particularly important in determining how many seats each state gets in the House of Representatives, and for population-based federal funding formulas ... critics have argued that the true purpose of the question was to mess with the results—either to benefit the Republican Party and red states or to advance the Trump administration's anti-immigration agenda.*
>
> *The widespread expectation was that the question would stoke fear among unauthorized immigrants and their family members, scaring off millions of mostly Latino residents from responding, and meaning states where those residents are concentrated will be undercounted. (Those states, which mostly favor Democrats, would then get smaller House of Representatives delegations and less federal funding because of the undercount.)[1]*
>
> 1. Andrew Prokop, "Trump's Census Citizenship Question Fiasco, Explained," *Vox*, modified July 11, 2019, www.vox.com/2019/7/11/20689015/census-citizenship-question-trump-executive-order.

summer months when desert temperatures can reach higher than 110 degrees Fahrenheit (43 degrees Celsius). Every year, hundreds of immigrants die or suffer dehydration and heat stroke due to exposure. Dr. Samuel Keim, an associate professor of emergency medicine at the University of Arizona, created an index to inform unauthorized immigrants which days were the most dangerous for attempting a border crossing. He knew that people were going to attempt the crossing whether they had that information or not, and his hope was to keep people from dying while doing it. "These people are dying on U.S. soil. This is a U.S. issue. It's not a Mexico issue,"[6] noted Keim.

The Mexican government issued an illustrated manual to notify border crossers of the dangers posed by the elements, and pro-immigration groups have voluntarily placed water stations along popular desert routes that unauthorized immigrants travel. Such actions have drawn criticism from groups that believe these actions only encourage illegal immigration.

Unauthorized immigrants are also at the mercy of smugglers, referred to as "coyotes" by the US Border Patrol. These smugglers take advantage of immigrants by charging high fees to aid them in crossing the border undetected. They have been known to leave border crossers lost in the desert or sell them into indentured servitude to dishonest business owners in the United States, who force unauthorized immigrants to work and live in terrible conditions. There's little choice for immigrants in these situations because they fear that calling the police will lead to their own deportation.

Crossing the border between the United States and Mexico is dangerous. People walk for miles in high temperatures, with no access to food or water.

Taking Risks for Opportunities

Getting to America is a great ordeal for many immigrants, and many who arrive continue to face tough situations. Immigrants are often treated like criminals by the media and the government, making everyday life much harder for them. The unfortunate truth is that many concerns about crime are directed at Latinx immigrants. However, that doesn't necessarily mean these concerns are logical or true. The problem lies in a cyclical process that begins with education in many Latin American countries.

In Mexico, for example, primary and secondary education is statistically substandard in poorer areas of the country, and only those in the upper classes can afford to send their children to good schools. This means the rich stay rich and the poor stay poor because high-paying jobs generally require higher education. The poor then immigrate to America, and although the pay is much better than what they were making in Mexico, it's often minimum wage or lower, making social mobility as difficult as it was at home. Tuition at American colleges is prohibitively expensive, so few immigrants who find themselves in this position are able to go back to school.

In 2018, *USA Today* reported that, whether or not they have citizenship status, foreign-born immigrants are more likely to live in poverty than people born in the United States. Among the foreign-born population living in poverty, Latinx made up the largest group. In American popular culture, poverty and crime are often related, so the media regularly paints the entire immigrant population, especially Latinx, as criminals, pointing to isolated incidents and making a commentary about immigrants as a whole. The fact is that immigrants in the United States have never been more likely to commit a crime than native-born people; in fact, they're statistically much less likely to be involved in criminal activity, as a report from the American Immigration Council shows:

> *According to an original analysis of data from the 2010 American Community Survey (ACS) ... roughly 1.6 percent of immigrant males age 18–39 are incarcerated [put in jail], compared to 3.3 percent of the native-born. This disparity [difference]*

in incarceration rates has existed for decades, as evidenced by data from the 1980, 1990, and 2000 decennial censuses. In each of those years, the incarceration rates of the native-born were anywhere from two to five times higher than that of immigrants.

The 2010 Census data also reveals that incarceration rates among the young, less-educated Mexican, Salvadoran, and Guatemalan men who make up the bulk of the unauthorized population are significantly lower than the incarceration rate among native-born young men without a high-school diploma. In 2010, less-educated native-born men age 18–39 had an incarceration rate of 10.7 percent—more than triple the 2.8 percent rate among foreign-born Mexican men, and five times greater than the 1.7 percent rate among foreign-born Salvadoran and Guatemalan men.[7]

Many schools in Mexico are underfunded and overcrowded, making it hard for students to get a good education.

This, however, doesn't keep immigration policy from treating immigrants like criminals. With new policies directed specifically at immigrants in the name of safety, it's more difficult for immigrants to remain innocent in the eyes of the law. For example, the Illegal Immigration Reform and Immigrant Responsibility Act (IIRIRA) broadened the definition of a felony only in the case of immigrants so they could be deported for crimes that are considered misdemeanors, or minor crimes, for the native-born population. This, in turn, takes away opportunities for immigrants to find better jobs, make more money, and go to school, which would make it easier to find better jobs in the first place and give immigrants the chance to rise above the poverty line and no longer be profiled as criminals.

This kind of cyclical process is called institutionalized oppression—a system of mistreatment toward any particular social group that's supported and enforced by society and social institutions. Although there's no reason why immigrants shouldn't be able to achieve economic and social equality with native-born citizens in the United States, they're prevented from doing so simply because of their status as immigrants and the American cultural systems that keep them impoverished, poorly educated, and seen as criminals.

Your Opinion Matters!

1. How is the modern image of an immigrant changing?
2. Do you think immigration laws need to be reformed? If so, how?
3. Why are immigrants often looked down upon by society?

ECONOMIC IMPACTS

One major concern many opponents of illegal immigration have is the effect on the economy and, by extension, how Americans will be affected. They say undocumented immigrants are a drain on the economy, illegally using welfare benefits such as Medicaid and food stamps as well as taking advantage of the public school system—all while paying none of the taxes that support such systems. They also believe immigrants take jobs away from US citizens.

Most of these concerns have been proven false by various studies; the high proportion of immigrant labor, both authorized and unauthorized, in the workforce has actually had a positive impact on the US economy. By improving productivity, immigrant workers allow American businesses to grow, raising wages and increasing employment opportunities for people in similar positions. On top of this, immigrants often open businesses of their own and create jobs.

They also contribute by paying taxes; authorized or not, most immigrants file yearly income tax returns, hoping it will create a paper trail they can use to prove that they would be model citizens and provide a path for them to achieve that status. Even if they don't file a tax return, they generally end up paying income, sales, and property taxes. However, since

Many undocumented immigrants hold low-paying jobs that don't require college degrees. About 31 percent of drywall installers, similar to this man, are undocumented immigrants.

they don't have a legal Social Security number, they have no way to access welfare benefits.

One area that's clearly creating a drain on government resources is the increased cost of securing the southern US border and enforcing immigration laws that are being broken by unauthorized immigrants and the companies that hire them. Government representatives believe the increased security at the border and the stricter enforcement of immigration laws will decrease the amount the United States spends on immigrants, but the economic repercussions of kicking out and keeping out sources of tax money and cheap labor remains to be seen.

Paying Taxes and Receiving Benefits

The federal and state governments raise the money required to provide public services and benefits to the population by collecting taxes on income and the manufacture and sale of goods and private services. The poor are heavily reliant on public services, but poor individuals and families generally pay less in taxes because their income and purchasing power are lower. Critics of immigration have drawn the conclusion that unauthorized immigrants who fall into this category use too many government resources.

However, decades of research have proven this theory false. Most undocumented immigrants are not eligible to receive federal benefits, such as Medicaid and food stamps, except in emergency situations; for example, they may qualify in some places for emergency Medicaid if their life is in immediate danger. Legal permanent residents (LPRs), or immigrants who aren't citizens but have come to the country legally, aren't eligible for these benefits until they've been in the United States for at least five years. Some LPRs eventually become citizens, but others get their immigration documentation, or "green card," renewed every 10 years. Some states allow immigrants to access certain benefits, but this varies widely. Children who are born in the United States to unauthorized immigrants automatically gain citizenship and are eligible for all the benefits a citizen receives; however, their parents can't access the same services.

Research has also proven that immigrants—both authorized and unauthorized—pay far more in taxes than they receive in benefits. The situation has been clouded, however, by false statements. For example, Steven Camarota, director of research for the Center for Immigration Studies (CIS), a nonprofit think tank that tends to lean anti-immigration, noted, "On average, the costs that illegal immigrant households impose on federal coffers [funds] are less than half that of other households, but their tax payments are only one-fourth that of other households."[1] However, CIS was classified by the SPLC as a hate group in 2016 because many of its writers have pushed views that support white nationalism (the idea that the United States is only for white people) and anti-Semitism (hatred of Jewish people). The SPLC noted that many of CIS's reports have been proven false by less biased groups.

Additionally, in April 2019, President Donald Trump stated that illegal immigration costs US taxpayers $200 billion each year. However, experts have noted that even by conservative estimates, this number is too high. Furthermore, they say it's misleading to put a price tag on a person's worth or contributions. David Dyssegaard Kallick, the deputy director of the nonpartisan Fiscal Policy Institute, explained, "It's really hard to calculate anyone's 'net cost' or 'net benefit.' We all use all kinds of services, from roads to military protection. How do we apportion what part of that is something I or you or an immigrant use?"[2]

Multiple studies have proven that immigrants do, in fact, pay taxes. According to the National Immigration Forum:

> Both documented and undocumented immigrants pay more into public benefit programs than they take out. According to Institute on Taxation and Economic Policy, undocumented immigrants contribute an estimated $11.74 billion to state and local economies each year. However, undocumented immigrants are not eligible for many of the federal or state benefits that their tax dollars help fund.
>
> Additionally, a few states have completed studies demonstrating that immigrants pay more in taxes than they receive in government services and benefits. A study in Arizona found that the state's

Some people argue that since many immigrants live below the poverty level, the key to eliminating poverty in the United States is to limit immigration. Jared Bernstein, a senior fellow at the Center on Budget and Policy Priorities and former economist for the Obama administration, explained why this reasoning is faulty:

Not unlike the analysis of single parents and poverty, too much analysis of this question basically argues that since immigrants, especially non-citizens (i.e., not naturalized) tend to be poorer than natives, if we take them out of the mix, we'd have less poverty. True: in 2012 (most recent data) the poverty rate for native-born persons was 14.3 percent while that of the foreign-born was 19.2 percent.

But that's not much of an insight. Since you could say the same thing about any group with below average incomes, it's pretty much saying we'd have less poverty if only we had fewer poor people.[1]

1. Jared Bernstein, "Immigration and Poverty," *HuffPost*, modified December 6, 2017, www.huffpost.com/entry/immigration-and-poverty_b_4650580.

immigrants generate $2.4 billion in tax revenue per year, which more than offsets the $1.4 billion in their use of benefit programs. Another study in Florida estimated that … immigrants in the state pay nearly $1,500 more in taxes per capita [per person] than they receive in public benefits.[3]

"I feel it's my responsibility to pay," said construction worker Dionicio Quinde Lima, an unauthorized immigrant in Queens in New York City. "And if it helps me get papers, fine."[4] Lima and millions like him file income taxes with the Internal Revenue Service (IRS) with a taxpayer identification number that the IRS has given out since 1996 to encourage noncitizens—including unauthorized

Most immigrants pay taxes. They often have taxes taken out of their paycheck, just like everyone else who has a job, and they pay sales tax when they buy something at the store.

immigrants—to pay their taxes. The IRS doesn't ask about citizenship status and doesn't care. "We want your money whether you are here legally or not," stated former IRS Commissioner Mark W. Everson, "and whether you earned it legally or not."[5]

Some lawmakers are concerned about remittances, or cash payments that authorized and unauthorized immigrants send to relatives back home to help them economically. In total, the United States sent out about $148 billion in remittances in 2017. Critics of immigration resent remittances because it amounts to money taken directly out of the US economy for the benefit of other nations. However, remittances from America help grow the global economy by spreading out the wealth of the richest nation in the world and giving it to those who many need the money more, both on an individual level and an institutional one.

Finding Work

Immigrants rarely come to America to be idle, which fits well in a country that takes pride in a strong work ethic. "Immigrants play an

Latinx Business Owners and Consumers

Many in the business community believe immigrants do more good than harm for the economy. The large number of Latinx immigrants have brought with them exciting opportunities for companies looking to expand their consumer reach and increase their profits. In 2015 alone, Latinx consumers added $1.3 trillion to the US economy. That same year, Terry College's *Multicultural Economy Report* predicted that the spending power of the Latinx community could reach $1.7 trillion by 2020. Latinx-owned businesses in the United States are growing 15 times faster than the national average, and the total Latinx market in the United States ranks as the third largest Latinx economy in the world, followed only by the nations of Brazil and Mexico.

important part in the successful story of America's free-enterprise economy and our dynamic culture," noted Daniel Griswold, former director of Trade Policy Studies for the Cato Institute, a Washington, DC, policy organization that engages in scholarly research and advocacy of legislative proposals. "They gravitate to occupations where the supply of workers falls short of demand, typically among the higher-skilled and lower-skilled occupations."[6] In other words, instead of "stealing" jobs from Americans, immigrants fill in the gaps by taking jobs that would otherwise go unfilled.

Many immigrants have met the demand for low-skilled labor that the United States currently needs. The US Bureau of Labor Statistics reported that of the top 30 jobs with the largest expected growth between 2014 and 2024, over half require "short-term-on-the-job" training. These jobs are typically in service industries and include retail sales, food preparation, landscaping, janitorial work, and home assistance. This trend matches well with the native-born population, where the median age of American workers is rising and more are attaining college degrees than ever before in the nation's history. These older and more educated workers are less likely to pursue low-wage jobs in the service sector that immigrants are more likely to accept.

Some people fear that native-born, low-skilled workers could be priced out of the job market by immigrants willing to work longer hours at tougher jobs for less money. Recent studies, though, suggest that native-born and foreign-born workers are not competing for the same jobs. In an analysis released in 2015, the Urban Institute's Maria E. Enchautegui reported that native-born and immigrant workers without high school diplomas are very different from each other in the kinds of work they are willing or able to do, noting, "If undocumented immigrants become authorized to work in the United States, that still may not be enough to increase competition with natives for low-skilled jobs."[7]

Native-born Americans in this category work as cashiers, truck drivers, and janitors, while immigrants are more likely to take jobs as housekeepers, cooks, and agricultural workers. While some overlap does exist, native-born Americans and immigrants are generally not in competition with each other. Immigrants have also been proven to create jobs by putting more demand on our economy.

Skilled, highly educated immigrants also raise the GDP of the country, which is an indicator of economic success. According to Vivek Wadhwa, author of *The Immigrant Exodus: Why America Is*

Native-born workers are more likely than immigrants to look for work as cashiers.

Losing the Global Race to Capture Entrepreneurial Talent, "This is a big advantage that the U.S. has over other countries—it is attracting the cream of the crop of scientific and technical talent from all over the world. If you segregated the groups into the highly skilled versus average [skilled], you would see the disproportionate contribution they make to GDP."[8]

Taking Advantage of Immigrants

Like authorized immigrants, unauthorized immigrants will readily work for less money because for many, it's generally still more than they would receive for the same work in their native countries. However, they're often taken advantage of by companies that realize these workers aren't familiar with the rights and benefits that all workers are entitled to by US law. Companies also know that unauthorized immigrants almost never report workplace abuses for fear of being deported. These companies sometimes find workers through equally unprincipled labor brokers who seek out unauthorized immigrants and take part of their salary as a fee for finding them the job. "The [guest worker] program has been rife with abuses, even during the best of times," said Cindy Hahamovitch, a history professor at the College of William and Mary. "There will never be enough inspectors to check every labor camp, contract and field."[9]

Companies can only be penalized for hiring undocumented workers if they knowingly do so, which is difficult for prosecutors to prove when a labor broker is involved because the company can claim that it's the broker's responsibility to establish a worker's citizenship status. This behavior is especially common in the construction industry, where many companies work through labor brokers.

Companies that rely on cheap immigrant labor often reduce their costs by not offering wage and health benefits and by classifying their workers as independent contractors, which allows them to avoid checking immigration status and paying payroll taxes and workers' compensation. Additionally, legitimate businesses are at a disadvantage because companies that don't pay these benefits can offer their services at a lower price to public- and private-sector customers.

Undocumented immigrants make up about 5 percent of the American workforce, and many experts say the US economy would suffer greatly if they were all deported. For example, about half of all farm workers, 24 percent of housekeepers, and about 15 percent of all construction workers are undocumented. Contrary to claims that undocumented workers are shutting Americans out of these jobs, some of these industries are growing, yet many Americans are not competing for those jobs. For example, it's estimated that the housekeeping industry will need about 112,000 more workers by 2024 to meet the growing demand. If all undocumented workers doing those jobs were deported, this industry would face a huge labor shortage. Similarly, undocumented immigrants make up a large number of dairy farm workers. In an article published on the CBS News website, Mary Jo Dudley, the director of the Cornell Farmworker Program, wrote:

> In 2017 research conducted by the Cornell Farmworker Program, 30 New York dairy farmers told us that they turned to undocumented workers because they were unable to find and keep reliable U.S. citizens to do the jobs. That's in part because farm work can be physically demanding, dirty and socially denigrated [looked down upon] work. More importantly, it is one the most dangerous occupations in the U.S.
>
> A study commissioned by the dairy industry suggested that if federal labor and immigration policies reduced the number of foreign-born workers by 50 percent, more than 3,500 dairy farms would close, leading to a big drop in milk production and a spike in prices of about 30 percent. Total elimination of immigrant labor would increase milk prices by 90 percent.[10]

In 2006, the federal government began cracking down on companies that knowingly hired illegal immigrants. Highly publicized raids performed by Immigration and Customs Enforcement (ICE) in late 2006 and early 2007 led to arrest and deportation hearings for hundreds of unauthorized immigrants, and employers faced criminal penalties for hiring them. Since then, raids have become a

Most Americans don't want jobs on dairy farms, which is why the dairy industry relies heavily on undocumented workers.

seldom-used tactic in finding unauthorized immigrants and their employers, but they still take place. In Buffalo, New York, four Mexican restaurants owned by Sergio Mucino were raided in 2016. Mucino was arrested for harboring undocumented workers, as well as committing tax fraud by not reporting how much his restaurants earned.

Punishing employers is widely believed by immigration reform advocates to help deter illegal immigration. The thinking goes that if American companies face huge fines and the potential loss of their business, they will not readily hire illegal immigrants, which will dry up the job opportunities available. Those who continue to defend the hiring of unauthorized immigrants state that the low wages they accept keep consumer prices down and generate healthy profits for American companies.

The High Cost of Enforcement

Illegal immigration laws in the United States went largely unenforced for years. The number of people picked up illegally crossing the border was small in comparison to those who actually got through, and 98 percent of those arrested between 2000 and 2005 were never prosecuted, according to an Associated Press analysis of federal data.

Security at the border has become of much greater concern since the terrorist attacks of September 11, 2001, when close to 3,000 people were killed by members of the Islamist terrorist group al-Qaeda. Members of al-Qaeda hijacked passenger planes and crashed them into New York's World Trade Center, the Pentagon outside of Washington, DC, and a field near Shanksville, Pennsylvania. When it was revealed the terrorists responsible for the attack were all living in the United States illegally with expired student visas, many people concluded that America's immigration system was broken to the point of being a threat to national security. Policing the country's borders to prevent future attacks on American soil became a high priority for law enforcement.

No single fence lines either the Mexican or Canadian border. Borders are defined by a patchwork of fences, cameras, and sensors, and while government-employed agents patrol different parts of the borders, official border-crossing stations remain the most highly guarded parts. Because of the length of America's borders— 5,525 miles (8,892 km) of border with Canada and 1,933 miles (3,111 km) with Mexico—it's impossible to guard the whole thing at one time.

When Donald Trump campaigned for president, he promised to build one long wall across the entire border. He also promised that Mexico would pay for it, although the Mexican president said the country wouldn't submit to that order. Some people supported the wall because they believed it would improve border security and stop the flow of illegal drugs and guns as well as unauthorized immigrants. However, others have opposed it, saying that such a wall would be too expensive to build and maintain, would not have any measurable effect on the illegal drug and gun trades, and would not halt most illegal immigration. Additionally, environmental activists have expressed concern about the problems a continuous wall would cause for plants and wildlife in the area. As of 2020, $18.1 billion has been diverted from the military budget to build 101 miles (163 km) of border wall—far short of the 450 miles (724 km) Trump promised to complete by the end of his first term in office.

September 11, 2001,
heightened many
Americans' fears about
immigration. However,
most of these fears have
proven over time to
be unfounded.

The US government's budget for immigration enforcement totals more than the budgets of most of its other main law enforcement agencies combined, and that number has been rising exponentially. As of fiscal year 2019—the financial year, which always runs from October of the previous year to September of the current year (in this case, October 2018 to September 2019)—the budget for border patrol and ICE combined was $22.5 billion, which is 22 percent higher than the previous year's budget. In 2012, US Border Patrol employed more than 21,000 agents. With the lowest starting salary being $38,619 per year, the US government is paying at least $811 million to staff the Mexican and Canadian borders every year. Some of the rest is spent on prosecuting unauthorized immigrants.

Operation Streamline is a project started in 2005 to arrest and convict, rather than deport, border crossers. It has swamped courts in the Southwest with immigration-related cases, spending tax dollars to incarcerate people who were once simply deported. About $1.87 billion was spent in 2014 on the housing of imprisoned unauthorized immigrants, and $1.71 billion of that cost was shouldered by state taxes. Despite these high costs, experts say there's no evidence that the policy has had any effect on illegal immigration. Furthermore, many have raised concerns about subjecting immigrants to imprisonment and trials rather than deporting them.

The debate about what level of responsibility for controlling immigration lies with the federal government versus with the states is ongoing. There's also a debate on whether the responsibility of assimilating immigrants into society lies with Americans or with the immigrants themselves.

Your Opinion Matters!

1. Why do you think people believe that unauthorized immigrants don't pay taxes but do get welfare benefits?

2. What job do you want to have when you get older? Are undocumented immigrants competing for jobs in that industry?

3. Name some industries that would suffer if every undocumented immigrant were deported.

LIVING IN A NEW COUNTRY

Adjusting to life in a new country can be difficult, but most immigrants do so enthusiastically. Some completely shed their old customs in an effort to be more "Americanized." Others blend their old and new cultures in ways that suit them best. In the process, American culture is enriched as well. Americans enjoy food, music, and fashion from all over the world because of immigration.

The elements of this cultural exchange have changed over time with the addition of immigrants from different nations, but the principles of freedom, democracy, and individualism upon which the nation was founded remain unchanged. Immigrants are expected to adopt and preserve these principles, as well as learn the English language and American customs in a process called assimilation. "Immigrants were expected only to abide by the basic tenets of an unspoken 'assimilation contract': allegiance to the nation's democratic principles, respect for individualism and hard work and—yes—willingness to learn English and use it outside their homes,"[1] wrote Peter D. Salins, professor of political science at the State University of New York, Stony Brook, in *Reinventing the Melting Pot*.

Some people have feared that the assimilation contract Salins refers to would be broken, but such fears have always

Immigrants come to the United States because they want to be part of American society. Most embrace their new country's values and customs without giving up their identity.

Borders and Safety

Nearly all borders in the world have some kind of rules about who can cross, as well as when and where people can cross. However, some are stricter than others. Most people who say they support open borders in the United States mean they want the immigration rules to be relaxed.

People who support closed borders argue that open borders are dangerous. They worry about Americans' safety, especially from drugs and gang members, which are two of Trump's biggest stated reasons for wanting to build the border wall. He and his supporters have frequently mentioned MS-13, a gang that has a strong hold on certain Latin American countries. Many people expressed fears that immigration would allow MS-13 members to freely enter the United States and commit violence against Americans. However, supporters of open borders point out that multiple studies have shown that there is no direct link between immigration and crime, while others have shown that immigration reduces crime; Trump has stated that increased protection will prevent MS-13 members from sneaking into the country, when in fact the gang was actually formed in Los Angeles, California, in the 1980s; and MS-13, while dangerous and violent, is neither the biggest nor the most dangerous gang in the United States. According to José Miguel Cruz, director of

proven to be unfounded. Immigrants from many nations have become upstanding members of American society, even when native-born groups have treated them with prejudice and have attempted to prevent them from obtaining the rights of citizens.

A Changing Identity

"Historically the substance of American identity has involved four key components: race, ethnicity, culture (most notably language and religion), and ideology,"[2] wrote Harvard professor Samuel P. Huntington in his book *Who Are We?: The Challenges to America's National* research for the Kimberly Green Latin American and Caribbean Center at Florida International University (FIU):

> *in pointing to MS-13 to try to scare Americans into harsh new immigration restrictions, Trump is overstating the danger the gang poses here in the United States. Worse, by using the gang to demonize all Latino immigrants, Trump is building inner-city walls that alienate communities and risk making criminal organizations more powerful, both here and overseas ...*

> *MS-13 in the United States does not rule cities as it does in Central America (though Trump claimed it does). It has no official national leadership structure here and does not collude [make deals] with corrupt politicians to win elections.*[1]

Similarly, experts have explained that drugs enter the country in many ways other than through the US-Mexico border and that even the drugs that are brought in from Mexico are smuggled past border patrol agents at legal crossings, not through open parts of the border.

1. José Miguel Cruz, "Trump Is Wrong About MS-13. His Rhetoric Will Make It Worse," *Washington Post*, January 31, 2018, www.washingtonpost.com/news/posteverything/wp/2018/01/31/trump-is-wrong-about-ms-13-and-his-rhetoric-will-make-it-worse.

Identity. While America's heritage of free enterprise and democracy and its cultural language component of English have remained unchanged throughout its history, the racial, ethnic, and religious elements have evolved over many years.

The American identity at the time of the Declaration of Independence could be described as white; Western European, also sometimes called Anglo-Saxon; and Protestant. This group is sometimes referred to as WASPs. This remained unchanged until after the American Civil War, when two significant developments took place. Freed slaves were guaranteed basic civil rights by law, although institutionalized racism and segregation in the form of poll taxes, voting restrictions, and separate educational and health facilities kept black people from achieving equality for more than a century. Also, the addition of Catholics from Ireland and Jews from Eastern and Southern Europe, as well as immigrants from Asia, began to change the religious, racial, and ethnic composition of the country. Though America remains 60.5 percent white in its racial

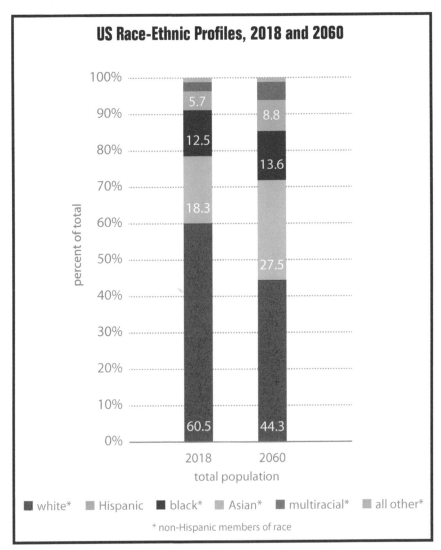

US Race-Ethnic Profiles, 2018 and 2060

percent of total

white*   Hispanic   black*   Asian*   multiracial*   all other*

* non-Hispanic members of race

total population

By 2060, no single race will be the majority (more than half) in the United States, as this information from the Brookings Institute shows.

composition, this percentage is continuously shrinking. The Brookings Institute has estimated that, based on census trends, less than half of the country will be white by 2045.

Huntington, a strong voice among opponents of open immigration, argued that American identity has not evolved but instead has been deliberately changed in favor of a multicultural identity. He wrote, "[Supporters of open immigration] encouraged immigrants to maintain their birth country cultures ... and denounced the idea of Americanization as un-American."[3] In Huntington's view, multiculturalism will ultimately harm America's identity because it divides people. He believes it doesn't offer the opportunity for celebrating the shared link of one overarching American identity; rather, it encourages ethnic groups to take strength from their differences. Huntington's views are generally shared by white nationalists, who are open about their desire to end immigration from majority nonwhite countries simply because they think the United States should be a whites-only country. These people have false ideas about people of color and believe white people are superior. Some anti-immigrant organizations, such as FAIR and CIS, have circulated white nationalist talking points—for example, claiming that most or all nonwhite immigrants are violent criminals—as their basis for wanting to limit immigration. The *Stanford Law Review* and the SPLC have noted that there's evidence to suggest that white nationalism has influenced the Trump administration's immigration policies.

Political science professors Luis R. Fraga and Gary M. Segura contradicted Huntington's views, asking, "How important is a single national culture for the preservation of democratic institutions?"[4] In their view, multiculturalism gives groups the ability to maintain their ethnic and cultural heritage while still participating in American society. They also cite examples of what they believe are successful democracies that have substantial ethnic and language diversity, including Spain, France, and India. Some attest that each of these nations has suffered political conflict among various ethnic or religious groups that has led to violence: Spain was engaged in a decades-long conflict with Basque separatists until 2011, France continues its struggle to accept its Muslim population, and India has

The Problem of White Nationalism

Many white nationalists claim to be against illegal immigration only, but the policies they support intentionally harm documented immigrants as well. The most extreme white nationalists openly advocate deporting everyone who isn't white, even if they're US citizens. The SPLC gave several examples of white nationalist goals, including repealing the part of the 14th Amendment that automatically grants citizenship to people who are born in the United States; limiting authorized immigrants' use of welfare programs; taking in fewer refugees who are fleeing violence in their home countries; supporting a policy of separating families at the border; and getting rid of the diversity visa lottery program, which grants visas to people from countries that are underrepresented in the US population.

Many experts say that white nationalism is the same as white supremacy, or the belief that white people are naturally better than people of color. White nationalists tend to deny being white supremacists, and experts generally agree that people with these views have changed the term because so many other people oppose the idea of white supremacy. As former senior Department of Homeland Security official John

a history of religious conflict between Hindus and Muslims. These issues, however, are comparable to the racial tension in America that spawned the Black Lives Matter movement. Anywhere cultures come together, there's bound to be conflict, but that fact doesn't make these places any less democratic or successful.

Generally, immigrants readily adopt American values, sometimes without realizing it. Boston College political science professor Peter Skerry noted that they even adopt American perspectives on themselves. He explained that many people who make up the Latinx community in the United States only think of themselves as Latinx because they're in America. They campaign for civil rights and fair treatment in America based on an identity that is unique to the United States.

Cohen explained, in the mind of a white supremacist, "We're going to try and frame it as a legitimate, ideological viewpoint that is connected to a belief in your country opposed to a belief in your race."[1]

It's worth noting that, while all white nationalists are racist, not all racists are white nationalists. For example, a racist may refuse to rent an apartment building to a black couple but wouldn't necessarily advocate deporting them or fear that the presence of a black person is a threat to white culture. In contrast, white supremacists spread the false belief that white culture is in danger of being erased by people of color, and white nationalists want people of color sent to other countries— even if it's a country that person has never set foot in. White nationalists generally try to convince others that diversity threatens the American way of life by making it impossible for Americans to be truly united.

1. Quoted in Elizabeth Thomas, "White Supremacy and White Nationalism Have Re-entered Our Political Conversation. But What Do They Mean?," ABC News, August 19, 2019, abcnews.go.com/Politics/white-supremacy-white-nationalism-entered-political-conversation/story?id=64998396.

Despite their differing views on the virtues of the American identity in an age of multiculturalism, opponents of open immigration such as Huntington and supporters of open immigration such as Fraga and Segura do want the American identity to evolve in a way that benefits all Americans. They just see that happening in different ways.

Latinx Assimilation

It's difficult to determine whether recent Latinx immigrants are actually assimilating into American society because assimilation is a process that takes place over generations, and many immigrants haven't been in the United States long enough to be fully assimilated. Assimilation, or lack of it, can only be determined by comparatively measuring, among other things, the extent of English language usage and the economic status of US-born children and grandchildren compared to that of their immigrant ancestors. Supporters of open immigration believe that when opponents such as Huntington argue that Latinx aren't assimilating, it's not only a premature assumption but also a false one. According to Gregory Rodriguez, writer and senior fellow of the pro-immigration group New America Foundation, Mexican Americans haven't attempted to build a parallel ethnic institutional structure and have never "shown much interest in distancing themselves from the mainstream … For example, in Los Angeles, home to more Mexicans than any other city in the U.S., there is not one ethnic Mexican hospital, college, cemetery or broad-based charity."[5]

The concern Huntington and other opponents of open immigration express about the perceived lack of assimilation was commonly voiced in the past when large waves of German immigrants came to America in the 19th century, but that has changed. As of 2017, the Hispanic population in the United States was 58.9 million, or 18.1 percent of the total US population. By way of comparison, about 46 million people—about 15 percent of the population—claim German ancestry. Because not all Hispanics share a common culture or ethnicity, only a common language, this makes Germans the largest ethnic group in America, and they have been for decades. However, there has been no concern voiced by Huntington or any other advocates of controlled immigration about the high proportion of German Americans in the United States. While much is heard about the issues and concerns of the Latinx community, there is no vocal German American lobby that is petitioning for German rights, and there are no German American leaders advocating German issues. Politicians and the media don't talk about the German vote, where Democrats and Republicans alike want the Latinx vote. Furthermore, when Germans show cultural pride at events such as parades and Oktoberfest, people generally don't get upset and accuse Germans of not assimilating, the same way they do at events that showcase pride in Latin cultures. As the Los Angeles Times noted, "some U.S. citizens … fume when Mexican Americans display the Mexican flag at Cinco de

Many cities have festivals celebrating various ethnicities. However, people of color tend to get the most backlash about this. For example, on St. Patrick's Day, people celebrate their Irish pride.

Mayo rallies"[6] because they see it as proof that Mexicans aren't loyal to the United States. Germans who wear traditional German clothing and wave German flags at their own cultural celebrations have no such problems. In fact, many people who aren't even German join in the celebrations.

Harvard history professor Stephan Thernstrom maintains that the reason there's no German American community that compares to the Latin American community in terms of political action and visibility is because Germans have assimilated into American culture. "There was a German ethnic group once, a huge and powerful one," Thernstrom wrote. "But having [ancestors] from Germany is not a significant indicator of how these people live and how they think of themselves."[7] During the high point of German immigration in the late 1800s, schools in Milwaukee, Wisconsin, which had the highest concentration of German immigrants in the country, taught students in German as well as English. Around 1900, there were 488 German-language newspapers dedicated to promoting German culture and identity. Today, there are sizable German American communities in cities across the United States, and there are festivals and parades in each of those cities that celebrate German heritage. However, that heritage is no longer the defining element of Americans of German descent living in the United States today. In fact, many people whose ancestors came from Germany, just like many other people of various ethnic backgrounds in the United States, consider themselves fully American and oppose letting other immigrants into the country.

Evidence suggests that Latinx will eventually follow in the footsteps of the Germans. While cultural heritage remains important, many second-generation immigrants never learn to speak Spanish. Although some immigrants encourage their children to learn the language, English quickly becomes the norm in immigrant households after more than one generation has grown up in America. "The newest generations of immigrants are assimilating into American society as fast and broadly as the previous ones," Julia Preston of the *New York Times* wrote in an article about a report on immigrant acculturation, "with their integration increasing over time 'across all measurable outcomes.'"[8]

Like German immigrants in the 1800s, Latinx immigrants tend to concentrate in certain areas; California, New York, Texas, and Florida are destinations of choice because they already have large Latinx populations. Ethnic enclaves, which are communities made up of distinct ethnic groups, are not unique in the immigrant experience, since strangers in a strange land will often gravitate toward what's familiar to feel safer. Similarly, many other countries have small American enclaves. However, no other immigration wave has had such a high percentage of people who speak the same language and identify themselves by their language, and the large populations in the Latinx enclaves add to the concern that assimilation will be slowed or not take place at all.

More than 50 Chinatowns exist in cities across the United States. These ethnic enclaves haven't prevented most Chinese immigrants from assimilating into American culture.

People concerned with the lack of assimilation among Latinx immigrants believe that within these tight-knit communities, where all the basic necessities of life can be provided by familiar faces speaking Spanish, there's little need to reach out and interact with the broader population. The regional concentration of immigrants may be changing, though, as statisticians—people who study statistics—have noted that immigrants have been dispersing to other areas, suggesting that Latinx immigrants are integrating into and becoming accepted in traditionally native-born American communities.

A further sign that assimilation is taking place is the rising level of American identity among Latinx. A 2017 Pew Research Center survey that inquired how Latinx or Hispanic people preferred to identify revealed that while 97 percent of foreign-born Latinx identified first as Hispanic, this number decreased across generations. By the fourth generation, only 50 percent of people with Hispanic ancestry self-identified primarily as Hispanic. The Pew Research Center noted that the two factors most responsible for this are a high rate of intermarriage between Latinx and other races as well as declining Latinx immigration rates.

Naturalization

For documented immigrants, becoming an American citizen—a process called naturalization—mainly consists of jumping through the government's hoops. "To become a U.S. citizen," the *Washington Post* explained, "a legal permanent resident must be at least 18; have lived in the United States continuously for five years; be able to speak, read, write and understand basic English; pass a background check; demonstrate knowledge of U.S. government and history, and swear allegiance to the United States."[9] Becoming a citizen gives immigrants the right to vote and the right to receive aid from government programs, and it also ensures that they cannot be deported. Their children, too, will be US citizens even if they're born in another country.

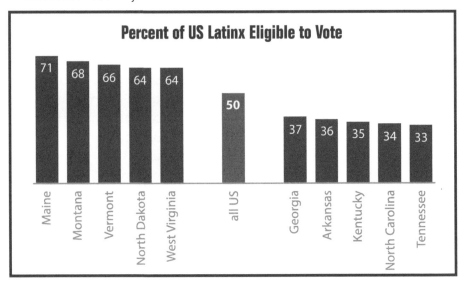

Percent of US Latinx Eligible to Vote

Only half of all Latinx who live in the United States are eligible to vote, although certain states have higher shares of eligible Latinx voters than others, as this information from the Pew Research Center shows. One major reason for this low percentage is that many American Latinx are under 18.

About half of all immigrants eventually become American citizens. Among the countries of origin with the highest rates of naturalization are Vietnam, Russia, the Philippines, and Korea, with Mexico, Guatemala, and Honduras among those with the lowest. When asked why they don't become citizens, many authorized Mexican immigrants expressed worries about not being proficient enough in English and failing the citizenship test, as well as about the $725 application fee. Twelve percent said they just hadn't gotten around to it.

Learning a New Language

While Latinx have a comparatively lower tendency toward naturalization than other immigrant groups, they're by and large following traditional patterns of absorbing the English language. Generally, immigrants follow a pattern in which the foreign-born first generation overwhelmingly either speaks only their native language or is bilingual, speaking both English and their native language. The second generation tends to be mainly bilingual, and the third generation speaks English almost exclusively with little, if any, use of their native language. A study of two decades' worth of census data by University of California, Berkeley, professors Jack Citrin, Amy Lerman, and Michael Murakami and University of Minnesota professor Kathryn Pearson determined that "Mexican immigrants may know less English than newcomers from other countries when they arrive in the United States, but … their rate of linguistic assimilation [the rate at which they learn English] is on par with or greater than those of other contemporary immigrant groups."[10]

According to a 2017 Pew Research Center report, 61 percent of foreign-born Hispanic immigrants had Spanish as their primary language, while 32 percent were bilingual and 7 percent spoke mainly English. The second generation demonstrated a marked improvement in English language ability, with 6 percent speaking only Spanish, 51 percent speaking Spanish and English equally, and 43 percent speaking only English. By the third generation, 75 percent considered English to be their primary language, and the remainder were bilingual. This level of change in only one generation shows there's little need for concern about the prevalence of Spanish-language media and advertising affecting linguistic assimilation in the United States.

Bilingual Classrooms versus English Immersion

In order for immigrant children to have the tools they need to succeed later in life, it's essential that they learn to speak English proficiently. However, there's an ongoing debate as to the best way to teach English in America's public schools, with supporters of bilingual education squaring off against supporters of English language immersion.

Bilingual education is a program that starts out by teaching elementary school students in their native language, with gradually increased exposure to English as they move through the school system. Supporters of bilingual education claim it allows children to gain literacy and fundamental knowledge in subjects such as math and science in their native language before tackling English literacy and proficiency. This prevents them from falling behind in other school subjects while maintaining cultural ties to their native heritage.

English language immersion is a program in which children are taught English from an early stage in their educational development. They're also instructed in the fundamentals of math and science in English, thereby allowing them to achieve English proficiency at a faster rate. Supporters of English language immersion state that students more readily grasp both English and other subjects, and they assimilate faster than they would with bilingual education.

The California public school system, which has more Hispanic students than any other school system in the country, has experimented with both programs, and there are teachers and parents who passionately support one program or the other. Some programs combine the two by hiring English immersion teachers who can speak the students' native language if they need help understanding a concept. However, there's a growing body of scientific research supporting bilingual education. The problem, according to non-profit education researcher The Hechinger Report, is that not all bilingual programs are executed effectively. Every student is different, and what works for one may not work for all. Furthermore, not all situations are the same. For example, in classrooms where the students speak only two languages, such as Spanish and English, it may make sense to switch between the two. In others, where children are immigrants from multiple different countries, this is not likely to be as effective. If bilingual education programs become widespread across the United States, they will need to be tailored specifically to the children they're for, meaning they'll be different from city to city and possibly even from school to school.

Your Opinion Matters!

1. What do you think it means to be an American?
2. What benefits are there to becoming a US citizen?
3. What are the advantages of bilingual education versus English language immersion?

THE FIGHT CONTINUES

Ever since the United States became a country and people started thinking of themselves as Americans rather than as a collection of immigrants or colonists, some people have wanted to limit immigration. For equally as long, others have pushed back against this mentality, reminding them that open immigration allowed them to become Americans in the first place. Instead of dying down over time, this fight has grown fiercer, especially after the September 11, 2001, terrorist attacks and again after the 2016 presidential election.

During the Obama administration, the country's immigration policy was strongly enforced, resulting in the removal of about 2.9 million people—the most deported under any president. The majority of these people were apprehended directly at the border, the place where most of the enforcement was concentrated, and instead of simply being informally tossed back over the way they had been for so long, they were arrested and formally deported. Obama's immigration enforcement was controversial because of the amount of money it cost to formally prosecute unauthorized immigrants, as well as because of what seemed to be racial profiling happening in immigrant investigations in the interior.

Stirring up more controversy was the Deferred Action for Childhood Arrivals (DACA) program. This program protects unauthorized immigrants brought into America as children by

Supporters and opponents of immigration both believe their view is what's best for the United States.

their parents, taking into account that the children didn't choose to immigrate illegally. It was created through an executive order—a document issued by the president that functions as a law—signed by Obama when Congress didn't pass the Development, Relief, and Education for Alien Minors (DREAM) Act. The DREAM Act was a law that, if passed, would have helped unauthorized immigrants get important documents such as work permits, a Social Security number, a driver's license, and a green card (authorization to stay in the country on a long-term basis). The DACA program prevents unauthorized immigrants who came to the United States as children, sometimes called "Dreamers" because of the DREAM Act, from being deported and gives them the right to apply for the same documents as the DREAM Act, with the exception of a green card. DACA is not popular among conservatives, even though it doesn't grant citizenship or even promise a path to citizenship. Because of this, Trump's administration has been working to repeal it. In November 2019, the Supreme Court heard oral arguments from lawmakers for and against DACA and announced that it would issue a final ruling

Shown here are three Dreamers speaking to their mothers through the US-Mexico border fence. Because of DACA, these three were able to remain in the United States, but their parents were deported.

sometime in 2020. A similar policy called Deferred Action for Parents of Americans (DAPA) aimed to keep families together by giving undocumented immigrants who had had children in the United States—making those children US citizens by default—a path to citizenship. DAPA was ended by the Trump administration in June 2017.

Despite the recent administrative attempts to fix America's current immigration policy, neither side of the argument has been appeased. Conservatives want to see stricter laws put in place to deport immigrants and keep immigrants out of the country. Some people say they don't care if immigrants come here, as long as they do it the "right" way. Many liberals want to see immigrants welcomed and no longer unnecessarily criminalized. Both sides wish to see major reform in the future, but how to get there, and how to agree, remains in question.

Changes from the Trump Administration

Although Democrats and Republicans agree that maintaining national security and fixing the economy are of the utmost importance, they have vastly different opinions about how those goals should be accomplished with regard to immigration. Democrats tend to lean liberally, pushing for more open immigration policies to stimulate the economy. They also oppose deportation because it separates mixed-status families—for instance, by deporting a noncitizen parent while allowing their American-born children to stay in the country—and sometimes results in people being sent "back" to a country they've never seen. If someone was brought to the United States as a baby, they won't remember anything about the country their parents came from. Deporting them to that country, many liberals argue, would be like forcing a German American whose ancestors immigrated in the 1800s to move to Germany. For these reasons, many Democrats favor creating a path to citizenship for undocumented immigrants rather than deporting them.

Republicans tend to lean conservatively, working to stop the flow of immigration from less prosperous nations and remove as many unauthorized immigrants from the United States as possible.

With such contrasting views, Democrats and Republicans often work against each other, aggressively blocking each other's policies in Congress and making government reform stagnate. Because of recent deadlock and frustration on both sides, the immigration debate became one of the main points of contention during the 2016 presidential election, aggravating the growing divide between parties. While immigration has been a deciding topic before, candidates have rarely been so polarized, or divided.

Democratic presidential nominee Hillary Clinton focused on a foundation of immigrants as individuals rather than a group and promised comprehensive plans to "fix the family visa backlog, uphold the rule of law, protect our borders and national security, and bring millions of hardworking people into the formal economy."[1] Supporting a path to citizenship, welcoming refugees, ending private immigrant detention centers, and upholding Obama's DACA program, Clinton represented a very liberal mindset when it came to immigration. She also believed that only immigrants who had a history of violence or criminal activity should be deported. This view, while well-intentioned, led some to worry about a broadening of the definitions of "violent" and "criminal" only when used to categorize unauthorized immigrants. Here, Clinton may have had to make changes in those definitions to shake the accusations of profiling, but her overall immigration policy was pleasing to most Democrats.

Republican presidential nominee Donald Trump fell on the opposite side of the spectrum, with extremely conservative views on immigration. After he was elected, his administration started making controversial changes to immigration policy. One of the first things he did after taking office was sign an executive order that included a 90-day ban on immigration from certain countries and a 120-day suspension of the US Refugee Admissions Program (USRAP). This travel ban became known as the "Muslim ban" because it affected people from countries where Islam is the main religion. The executive order never specifically mentioned the word "Muslim," but it did say that after the ban was lifted, the Department of Homeland Security would "prioritize refugee claims made by individuals on the basis of religious-based persecution, provided that the religion of the individual is a minority religion in the individual's country of nationality."[2] Since Islam is the majority religion in the affected countries, the order does mean that non-Muslims will be given preference. This has caused many people to call the travel ban unconstitutional since the United States has separation of church and state, which means laws aren't supposed to be made that give preference to any one religion.

The executive order was controversial in other ways as well. Critics called it racist and shared stories on social media of Syrian children—even those who had passed all the necessary entry requirements—in need of medical care who were sent back to their war-torn country, which was named in the travel ban. The American Civil Liberties Union (ACLU) called the travel ban a violation of people's rights and requested a stop to the executive order. After much back-and-forth in the court system and several changes to the wording of the travel ban, the Supreme Court upheld it on June 26, 2018. However, the ACLU won a case in February 2020 that caused the federal government to agree to

When Trump's travel ban first went into effect, hundreds of immigration lawyers across the country camped out at airports to offer legal help to incoming immigrants.

Concerns About Refugees

While Latin American immigration remains at the forefront of current social debates, immigration policy being debated in Congress is mostly focused on a different group: Middle Eastern refugees, especially those from Syria. At the beginning of 2011, civil war broke out in Syria, forcing thousands of Syrians into Jordan, Iraq, Lebanon, Turkey, Egypt, and eventually Germany, Sweden, and the United Kingdom (UK). By the end of 2016, with the war escalated by the terrorist organization ISIS, 4.8 million people had been displaced from their homes, fearing for their lives. The number of immigrants in the United States from the Middle East and North Africa region has doubled since the beginning of the new millennium due to the unstable political climate there, and as the situation worsens, more people seek safety every day. In October 2015, the Obama administration set a goal of taking in 10,000 refugees over the course of the fiscal year, a goal which it met a month early in late August 2016.

Even before the United States responded to the crisis in Syria, fear in America slowed the process of refugee immigration to a crawl. Critics claimed that terrorists were pretending to be refugees in order to gain access to the United States, and they expressed concerns about letting "just anyone" into the country. However, government officials have countered those claims by explaining the rigorous screening process:

All refugees of all nationalities considered for admission to the United States undergo intensive security screening involving

prioritize settling refugees, especially those who already have family members in the United States. Many individuals and organizations have vowed to continue to fight the ban, but for now it remains in effect.

A Crisis at the Border

Another Trump administration decision that has deeply divided the country was put into place after Trump declared that there was a *multiple federal intelligence, security and law enforcement agencies, including the National Counterterrorism Center, the FBI's Terrorist Screening Center, and the Departments of Homeland Security, State and Defense. Consequently, resettlement is a deliberate process that can take 18-to-24 months.*

Applicants to the U.S. Refugee Admissions Program are currently subject to the highest level of security checks of any category of traveler to the United States. These safeguards include biometric (fingerprint) and biographic checks, and a lengthy in-person overseas interview by specially trained DHS officers who scrutinize the applicant's explanation of individual circumstances to ensure the applicant is a bona fide refugee and is not known to present security concerns to the United States.[1]

Furthermore, multiple fact-checks and studies have proven that people's fears about terrorists posing as refugees are completely unfounded. Research shows that most terrorist attacks in the United States are carried out by native-born Americans, especially white supremacists.

1. "Testimony of Anne C. Richard, Assistant Secretary for the Bureau of Population, Refugees, and Migration to the House Judiciary Committee, Immigration and Border Security Subcommittee Hearing on 'The Syrian Refugee Crisis and Its Impact on the Security of the U.S. Refugee Admissions Program,'" House of Representatives Judiciary Committee, November 19, 2015, www.hsgac.senate.gov/imo/media/doc/Testimony-Richard-2015-11-19-REVISED1.pdf.

crisis at the US-Mexico border. The George W. Bush administration started a policy that has been widely known as "catch and release," although critics say this term is inaccurate as well as dehumanizing to immigrants by comparing them to animals. Under this policy, unauthorized immigrants who were caught at the border would be given a court date and some kind of monitoring system—for example, they might have to wear an ankle bracelet to track their movements or check in regularly with officials—then allowed into American society until their court date came months or sometimes later. The Obama administration continued to enforce this policy but created new guidelines that prioritized deporting immigrants with a history of gang membership or criminal activity.

The catch-and-release policy has been heavily criticized by conservatives, who claim that almost none of the released immigrants show up to their court dates and instead simply live illegally in the United States. Trump himself has claimed that only about 3 percent of immigrants come to their court date. However, data from the Department of Justice (DOJ) disproves this claim. The department's records show that about 75 percent of immigrants do, in fact, show up to court. According to Madhuri Grewal, federal immigration policy counsel for the ACLU, many of the remaining 25 percent "do not make their court dates because the government has made a mistake: There are many cases of immigrants being released with incorrect court dates or addresses."[3]

In an effort to address what Trump called the immigration crisis, the DOJ put a "zero tolerance" policy in place on May 7, 2018. This policy had already been in place in certain border areas, but the DOJ's announcement made it federal policy for the entire southern border. Any undocumented immigrants who were caught at the border, whether or not they were seeking asylum, were put into detainment centers made from converted warehouses. Opponents of the policy called the centers concentration camps. Journalists and lawmakers who toured the facilities reported that the conditions were inhumane. The warehouses were separated by metal fencing into a series of large cages. Instead of blankets and beds, detainees slept on the floor under large sheets, and they were often denied enough food and proper health care.

The part of the policy that caused the most outrage was the separation of children from their parents. In 1997, a court case that is now known as the Flores Settlement Agreement limited detainment of children to 20 days. This means families who are traveling together can't be detained indefinitely. In an effort to get around this limit, the Trump administration started separating families in April 2018; the children were released after 20 days, while the parents were detained until they could be prosecuted—sometimes for months. Opponents of this policy called it cruel, especially after videos went viral of caged children crying for their parents and babies being forcibly removed from their parents' arms. So many people protested against the family separation policy that the Trump administration first claimed it wasn't happening and then, on June 20, 2018, rescinded it, or took it back.

Although the policy only lasted two months, it has taken years to untangle the problems it caused. Poor records were kept on the status of the children who were released, so tracking them down to reunite them with their families has proven difficult; in fact, court documents say it could take up to two years to reunite all the families. Furthermore, the Trump administration has

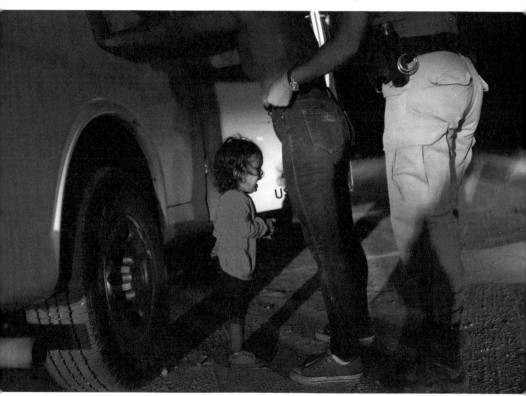

When a photo of this crying Honduran two-year-old went viral in 2018, it became a symbol of the tragedy of family separation. This child didn't end up being separated from her mom, but more than 2,000 others were.

reported to a federal court that some border patrol agents were still separating families despite the fact that the policy had been rescinded. Adults and children who are detained at the border are still suffering from poor conditions, causing physical and psychological problems, but former Homeland Security Secretary Kirstjen Nielsen has repeatedly lied, in tweets and before the House Judiciary Committee, about the policy, stating that the administration has never had a policy of separating families.

While the majority of Americans and others around the world strongly opposed the Trump administration's decisions, saying that they violated human rights, some defended them. They claimed that the threat of family separation would deter immigrants from trying to cross the border illegally; that conditions in the detainment centers weren't bad and were, in fact, nicer than the homes immigrants had in their own countries; that the Obama administration was the one that instituted the family separation policy; that family separation was a necessary consequence of the Flores Settlement Agreement; and that separating children from the adults accompanying them was safer for the children because there was no guarantee that the adults they were with were actually their parents. Many people believed that Latinx gang members were stealing children so they could pose as families to gain entry to the United States and sell the children into slavery. Every single one of these claims has repeatedly been proven false. As of 2020, this issue is still very much in the public consciousness. For instance, the Super Bowl halftime show that year featured young backup singers sitting in large, neon, cage-like structures—a reference to the children being caged at the border.

In September 2019, the Trump administration announced that it would end the catch-and-release policy, replacing it with one that has come to be known as Remain in Mexico. Immigrants caught at the border who don't claim asylum will be immediately sent back to their home country. Those who do claim asylum will be forced to wait for their trial in Mexico—a decision experts say keeps these immigrants in danger. That same month, the United States signed an agreement with El Salvador in which El Salvador agreed to let some immigrants seek asylum there instead of continuing on to the United States.

The 2020 Super Bowl halftime show, featuring Latina performers Jennifer Lopez and Shakira, included a politically charged visual message by showing children in cages.

Objections to ICE

The Trump administration is far from the first to put controversial immigration policies in place. US Immigration and Customs Enforcement (ICE) was founded in March 2003, during President George W. Bush's first term in office, by the then-new Department of Homeland Security, replacing the Immigration and Naturalization Service (INS). According to the ICE website, the agency's mission "is to protect America from the cross-border crime and illegal immigration that threaten national security and public safety."[4] ICE is known for its extensive raids, the results of which have been about 1.5 million deportations from the interior of the country (as opposed to at the border) during the Obama administration. By primarily going after unauthorized immigrants who have missed deportation hearings, those with connections to terrorist organizations, and those with criminal records, supporters of ICE say it works to remove immigrants who may be threats to national safety.

Critics of the organization, however, believe many of the deportations that have taken place were not warranted. Some worry about the grounds on which unauthorized immigrants are arrested and deported, claiming that many are deported on technicalities and without regard for individual circumstances:

> As proof that it is weeding out the "bad guys," Immigration and Customs Enforcement (ICE) recently reported that 59 percent of deportations in fiscal year 2013 involved noncitizens with criminal records. Yet, what ICE did not highlight is that the vast majority of criminal deportees were expelled for non-violent offenses, with 60 percent convicted of misdemeanors punishable by less than one year in prison …

> "Smart enforcement" strategies have led to an unprecedented level of cooperation between ICE, the FBI and local police agencies as they seek to target "terrorists" and "criminal aliens." Not surprisingly, the proportion of criminal to non-criminal deportations has grown steadily [over] the past decade. Yet, we have seen national declines in crime rates over the same period, and studies have shown that immigrants are much less likely than US citizens to commit crimes. Immigrants are not becoming more unlawful or dangerous; the government is just more aggressive in labeling them as such.[5]

Some advocates for immigrant rights maintain that these raids are just excuses to conduct mass deportations of hardworking people who are immigration violators but do not pose a danger to the public. "They're trying to sell it as something where they target (criminals) but it's become part of a larger dragnet,"[6] said Pedro Rios, director of the American Friends Service Committee in San Diego, California.

Immigrant arrests that break up families have also been a focus of concern. In 2017, the Center for American Progress estimated there were 16.7 million people living in mixed-status families in the United States where at least one member was in the country illegally. Raids that round up immigration violators have the potential to take fathers and mothers away from their children, and vice versa. In these situations, unauthorized immigrants have the right to make their circumstances known to immigration judges, who make the final decision about whether or not to deport individuals. Due to an extensive case backlog, potential deportees can remain in legal limbo for months, which creates an agonizing emotional situation while their fates are decided.

By definition, all unauthorized immigrants have, in fact, broken the law because they are violators of immigration regulations. Pro-immigration-control groups believe it's unfair to allow unauthorized immigrants opportunities available to authorized immigrants and citizens who have obeyed all the laws, including immigration regulations. However, since the vast majority of unauthorized immigrants are otherwise law-abiding people whose only desire is to find better jobs than were available in their native countries, many supporters of immigration are willing to forgive their violations. They also don't see the reason for the nationwide sweeps being conducted by ICE. In their view, if immigrants are working hard and obeying the law, they should be afforded some of the rights available to citizens because they're contributing to the prosperity of the American economy.

Furthermore, criticism of ICE has been growing since 2016, as claims of abuses by ICE employees have become more commonly

Only about 35 percent of Americans oppose ICE, but ICE's opposition has been much more visible than its supporters.

reported. News outlets have reported ICE officials mocking crying children, refusing detained immigrants health care, acting violently toward detained immigrants, and committing other violations. Such reports have turned some of the American public against the organization, fearing it has become less a tool for national security and more a program for targeting people the government deems undesirable. In an article for the nonprofit organization Human Rights Watch, Grace Meng wrote that the main effect of ICE raids "will be to foster cruelty and terror with the apparent aim to deter others from seeing refuge or a better life in the US."[7] To opponents of immigration, this is a good thing; they believe that coming down hard on current unauthorized immigrants will make other immigrants too scared to come to the United States. To supporters of

Understanding Islamic Terms

With Islamist extremist groups terrorizing the Middle East and the rest of the world, politicians and media outlets have begun discussing Sharia law, or the law according to the Quran, the Islamic holy book. Islamic is a word that means relating to Islam; Islamist is the term for fundamentalists who twist the religion and use it as an excuse to commit acts of violence. ISIS is an Islamist group because it claims to uphold Sharia law, using it as justification for the torture, mutilation, and murder of nonbelievers—a fact that has caused concern among some because of the large number of Muslim immigrants America takes in. Some people reason that, since Sharia law is Islamic law, and ISIS commits atrocities in the name of Sharia law, then Islam must be an evil religion. Some even fear that Muslim immigrants will follow Sharia law rather than the laws of the United States. However, all of these assumptions are false. ISIS does not interpret Sharia law the way most Muslims do; instead, the group uses it to falsely justify their evil actions. Similarly, the Christian Bible contains many violent passages, but only extremist groups believe those passages are meant to be taken literally. Carol Kuruvilla, an associate religion editor for *HuffPost*, explained:

immigration, this harms both the United States and immigrants who are fleeing danger in their home countries. This environment of fear also harms immigrants by making them less likely to report crimes, send their children to school, and seek medical care because those things could all alert ICE to their presence. As with Obama's policy of criminalizing immigration, ICE raids also place a large and expensive burden on the US prison system.

A Safe Haven

To combat what many see as abuse by the government, some cities have identified themselves as sanctuary cities. This means they protect undocumented immigrants by limiting cooperation with law enforcement agencies such as ICE. Sanctuary cities don't

Sharia ... encompasses both a personal moral code and a general religious law that can influence the legal systems of Muslim-majority countries. It's also a living body of law—it developed over the centuries and is still being examined with fresh eyes by Muslim scholars and believers today ...

[Scholar Qasim] Rashid writes, "The most 'Muslim country' in the world is likely America, because America guarantees freedom of religion, freedom of speech, freedom of expression and freedom of thought—all hallmarks of Shariah [Sharia] Law. Those nations that oppress in the name of Shariah are as justified in their claims, as the slave owners who claimed their right to slavery was based on the Bible."

You do NOT need to worry about Sharia dominating American life and courts. Because nothing trumps the U.S. Constitution. No national Muslim organization has ever called for Sharia to supercede American courts. It's completely beside the point of Sharia and it's not something American Muslims want.[1]

1. Carol Kuruvilla, "5 Things You Need to Know About Sharia Law," *HuffPost*, modified January 31, 2017, www.huffpost.com/entry/5-facts-you-need-to-know-about-sharia-law_n_5788f567e4b03fc3ee507c01.

report undocumented immigrants to the federal government when they're arrested and charged with minor crimes. Many cities made this decision because they realized that when immigrants were deported after being arrested for minor crimes, the trust between local police and immigrant communities was broken. The threat of being deported kept unauthorized immigrants from reporting crimes against them. This allowed criminals to remain free to prey on other members of the community, creating a bigger public safety risk than the crimes most immigrants were being charged with—mainly traffic violations and other nonviolent misdemeanors. Chicago; Los Angeles; New York; Boston, Massachusetts; Seattle, Washington; New Orleans, Louisiana; and San Francisco, California, are just a few of the American sanctuary cities.

Trump has vowed to defund sanctuary cities to force them to comply. This would leave major cities across the country with no budget with which to fund social services. City government officials, however, doubt he would make such a move, and they have stated that they will not be giving up their unauthorized immigrants.

The Role of Racism

Although many claim that immigration issues are purely economic, race and religion play a role as well. America has a long history with prejudice and racism, and while some think racism is no longer a concern, racially fueled politics continue to this day.

In times of global crisis, immigrants have consistently carried the weight of America's tendency toward prejudice. During World War II, for instance, Japanese immigrants and their American-born children were put in internment camps after Pearl Harbor was attacked, and the government refused to take in Jewish refugees fleeing the Nazis for fear that some of them might be German spies. In the 21st century, as the United States struggles with economic ups and downs and as terrorist attacks occur around the world, the country once again points fingers at immigrants; according to some, Latinx ruined the economy and Syrian refugees are all potential terrorists. In a poll by Morning Consult, a nonpartisan media and technology company, about 53 percent

Nonwhite immigrants receive much more hatred than white ones. In 2018, when hundreds of Central Americans traveled together to the United States to seek asylum, many people expressed fears about the safety of letting these immigrants into the United States. Such fears are virtually never expressed about white immigrants.

of American voters believe Middle Eastern immigrants have a negative effect on American society, despite there being no evidence to support that belief, and about 38 percent believe the same about Latinx. These beliefs are most common among white voters.

This isn't to say that everyone who opposes immigration is racist, but the evidence suggests a racial bias in Americans—specifically in white Americans—against those of Latin American, Middle Eastern, and African origin. Whether or not people realize it, their culture shapes the way they think about themselves in relation to others, and America's mainly white, Christian-geared media gives the illusion that white, Christian people are the cultural default. Therefore, when white Americans look out at the rest of the world, they see many people who don't look like them or believe the same things as them and deem them "wrong." In the case of immigration,

Americans worry that immigrants will challenge the country's values and make America worse in some way.

After Trump was elected president, the number of hate crimes against nonwhite people—citizens and noncitizens alike—rose dramatically. Muslim women have reported being screamed at for wearing a hijab (a religious headscarf) and having their hijabs pulled off by people calling them terrorists. Even children have experienced the negative impact of racism. In a survey of teachers by the Southern Poverty Law Center, "more than two-thirds of the teachers … reported that their students—mainly Muslims, immigrants and children of immigrants—were worried about what could happen to them and their families after the November [presidential] election. And more than one-third of the teachers said they've noticed a rise in anti-immigrant and anti-Muslim sentiment among their students as well."[8] Even documented immigrants have expressed such fears.

An Uncertain Future

With immigration policy changing rapidly and xenophobia on the rise, many people are uncertain about what the future of immigration will look like for the United States. Republican politicians will likely continue aggressively targeting undocumented immigrants. Recent Democratic politicians have expressed more of a desire to work toward providing a path to citizenship than to deport and limit immigration. However, these things aren't set in stone, and politicians can certainly have views that differ from those of their party. With Americans more deeply politically divided than ever before, it's difficult to predict how any arrangement that makes both sides happy might be reached.

Your Opinion Matters!

1. What are arguments for and against unauthorized immigrants remaining in the country?
2. Why have some cities become sanctuary cities?
3. What predictions do you have for the future of immigration?

GETTING INVOLVED

The following are some suggestions for taking what you've just read and applying that information to your everyday life.

- Learn more about the government's immigration policies so you can decide which ones you agree or disagree with.

- Ask a parent or guardian to take you to a protest about immigration issues.

- Double check anything you read or hear about immigration to make sure it's not fake news designed to scare you.

- Ask your friends and family members who are over 18 to consider voting for politicians whose views on immigration you support.

- Donate some of your money to organizations that are working to help reunite the families who were separated at the border.

- Learn more about immigrants, their stories, and their cultures.

- If you hear people saying false things about immigration, politely correct them.

- Volunteer your time with organizations that help immigrants.

- If you see anyone, including immigrants, being bullied in your school or neighborhood, step in and defend them.

- Support businesses in your community run by immigrants.

NOTES

Introduction: A Controversial Subject

1. Quoted in Peter Prengaman, "Immigrant-Rights Marches Decline in Size and Spirit," *Philadelphia Inquirer*, May 2, 2007, www.inquirer.com/philly/news/special_packages/inquirer/immigration_debate/20070502_Immigrant-rights_marches_decline_in_size_and_spirit.html.

2. Quoted in Daniel Gonzalez, "Marchers Re-Energized Amid Immigration Push," *Arizona Republic*, May 2, 2007.

Chapter One: A Brief History of Immigration

1. "Immigrant," *Merriam-Webster*, accessed February 28, 2020, www.merriam-webster.com/dictionary/immigrant.

Chapter Two: New Millennium, New Immigration Patterns

1. "About Hispanic Origin," US Census Bureau, modified March 7, 2018, www.census.gov/topics/population/hispanic-origin/about.html.

2. Leah Nelson, "How Do We Know FAIR Is a Hate Group?," Southern Poverty Law Center, August 10, 2012, www.splcenter.org/hatewatch/2012/08/10/how-do-we-know-fair-hate-group.

3. Ted Hesson, "Why American Cities Are Fighting to Attract Immigrants," *The Atlantic*, July 21, 2015, www.theatlantic.com/business/archive/2015/07/us-cities-immigrants-economy/398987.

4. "Why Don't Immigrants Apply for Citizenship?," American Immigration Council, modified November 25, 2019, www.americanimmigrationcouncil.org/research/why-don%E2%80%99t-they-just-get-line.

5. Cecilia Muñoz, "The Myth of Chain Migration," *Politico Magazine*, January 26, 2018, www.politico.com/magazine/story/2018/01/26/myth-chain-migration-trump-family-immigration-216536.

6. Quoted in Michael Martinez, "At 104 Degrees, the Forecast Is Death," *Chicago Tribune*, March 18, 2007, www.chicagotribune.com/news/ct-xpm-2007-03-18-0703180177-story.html.

7. Walter Ewing, Daniel E. Martínez, and Rubén G. Rumbaut, "The Criminalization of Immigration in the United States," American Immigration Council, July 13, 2015, www.americanimmigrationcouncil.org/research/criminalization-immigration-united-states.

Chapter Three: Economic Impacts

1. Steven A. Camarota, "The High Cost of Cheap Labor," Center for Immigration Studies, August 25, 2004, cis.org/Report/High-Cost-Cheap-Labor.

2. Quoted in Debbie Lord, "Immigration: Can Undocumented Immigrants Get Federal Public Benefits?," Boston 25 News, modified April 4, 2019, www.boston25news.com/news/trending-now/immigration-can-undocumented-immigrants-get-federal-public-benefits/936951998.

3. "Fact Sheet: Immigrants and Public Benefits," National Immigration Forum, August 21, 2018, immigrationforum.org/article/fact-sheet-immigrants-and-public-benefits.

4. Quoted in Nina Bernstein, "Tax Returns Rise for Immigrants in U.S. Illegally," *New York Times*, April 16, 2007, www.nytimes.com/2007/04/16/nyregion/16immig.html.

5. Quoted in Bernstein, "Tax Returns Rise for Immigrants in U.S. Illegally."

6. Daniel Griswold, "Mexican Migration, Legalization, and Assimilation," Cato Institute, October 5, 2005, www.cato.org/publications/speeches/mexican-migration-legalization-assimilation.

7. Maria E. Enchautegui, "Immigrant and Native Workers Compete for Different Low-Skilled Jobs," Urban Intitute, October 13, 2015, www.urban.org/urban-wire/immigrant-and-native-workers-compete-different-low-skilled-jobs.

8. Quoted in "What Migration Can (and Can't) Do for a Country's GDP," Wharton School, September 9, 2013, knowledge.wharton.upenn.edu/article/what-migration-can-and-cant-do-for-a-countrys-gdp.

9. Quoted in Steven Greenhouse, "Low Pay and Broken Promises Greet Guest Workers," *New York Times*, February 28, 2007, www.nytimes.com/2007/02/28/us/28labor.html.

10. Mary Jo Dudley, "These U.S. Industries Can't Work Without Illegal Immigrants," CBS News, modified January 10, 2019, www.cbsnews.com/news/illegal-immigrants-us-jobs-economy-farm-workers-taxes.

Chapter Four: Living in a New Country

1. Peter D. Salins, "The Assimilation Contract: Endangered but Still Holding," in Tamar Jacoby, ed., *Reinventing the Melting Pot: The New Immigrants and What It Means to Be American* (New York, NY: Basic Books, 2004), p. 102.
2. Samuel P. Huntington, *Who Are We?: The Challenges to America's National Identity* (New York, NY: Simon & Schuster, 2004), p. 12.
3. Huntington, *Who Are We?*, p. 142.
4. Luis R. Fraga and Gary M. Segura, "Culture Clash? Contesting Notions of American Identity and the Effects of Latin American Immigration," *Perspectives on Politics* 4, no. 2 (2006): p. 281.
5. Gregory Rodriguez, "Mexican Americans Are Building No Walls," *Los Angeles Times*, February 29, 2004, www.latimes.com/archives/la-xpm-2004-feb-29-op-rodriguez29-story.html.
6. Times Editorial Board, "Editorial: The Problem of Dual Citizenship," *Los Angeles Times*, December 26, 2014, www.latimes.com/opinion/editorials/la-ed-dual-citizenship-20141228-story.html.
7. Stephan Thernstrom, "Rediscovering the Melting Pot: Still Going Strong," in Jacoby, ed., *Reinventing the Melting Pot*, p. 52.
8. Julia Preston, "Newest Immigrants Assimilating as Fast as Previous Ones, Report Says," *New York Times*, September 21, 2015, www.nytimes.com/2015/09/22/us/newest-immigrants-assimilating-as-well-as-past-ones-report-says.html.
9. Tara Bahrampour, "Study: Legal Mexican Immigrants Become U.S. Citizens at a Lower Rate Than Others," *Washington Post*, February 4, 2013, www.washingtonpost.com/local/study-legal-mexican-immigrants-become-us-citizens-at-a-lower-rate-than-others/2013/02/04/a3751d30-6f0a-11e2-ac36-3d8d9dcaa2e2_story.html.
10. Jack Citrin, Amy Lerman, Michael Murakami, and Kathryn Pearson, "Testing Huntington: Is Hispanic Immigration a Threat to American Identity?," *Perspectives on Politics* 5, no. 1 (2007): p. 35.

Chapter Five: The Fight Continues

1. "Immigration Reform," Office of Hillary Rodham Clinton, accessed February 28, 2020, www.hillaryclinton.com/issues/immigration-reform.

2. "Executive Order: Protecting the Nation from Foreign Terrorist Entry into the United States," The White House, January 27, 2017, www.whitehouse.gov/the-press-office/2017/01/27/executive-order-protecting-nation-foreign-terrorist-entry-united-states.

3. Jack Herrera, "What Is 'Catch and Release'?," *Pacific Standard*, March 20, 2019, psmag.com/news/what-is-catch-and-release.

4. "What We Do," US Immigration and Customs Enforcement, modified December 4, 2018, www.ice.gov/overview.

5. Alejandra Marchevsky and Beth Baker, "Why Has President Obama Deported More Immigrants Than Any President in US History?" *The Nation*, March 31, 2014, www.thenation.com/article/why-has-president-obama-deported-more-immigrants-any-president-us-history.

6. Quoted in "Bush Administration Is Out of Control," Fair Immigration Reform Movement, April 4, 2007, fairimmigration.org/press/bush-administration-is-out-of-control.

7. Grace Meng, "ICE Raids on US Immigrant Families Risk Serious Abuses," Human Rights Watch, July 12, 2019, www.hrw.org/news/2019/07/12/ice-raids-us-immigrant-families-risk-serious-abuses-0.

8. Christina Wilkie, "'The Trump Effect': Hatred, Fear and Bullying on the Rise in Schools," *HuffPost*, April 13, 2016, www.huffpost.com/entry/trump-effect-southern-poverty-law-center_n_570e8619e4b03d8b7b9f2836.

FOR MORE INFORMATION

Books: Nonfiction

Coan, Peter Morton. *Ellis Island Interviews: Immigrants Tell Their Stories in Their Own Words*. New York, NY: Fall River Press, 2015.

Osborne, Linda Barrett. *This Land Is Our Land: A History of American Immigration*. New York, NY: Abrams Books for Young Readers, 2016.

Otfinoski, Stephen. *Immigration & America*. New York, NY: Scholastic, 2018.

Pidcock-Reed, Heather. *Immigration*. Philadelphia, PA: Mason Crest, 2020.

Saedi, Sara. *Americanized: Rebel Without a Green Card*. New York, NY: Alfred A. Knopf, 2018.

Books: Fiction

Jaramillo, Ann. *La Línea*. New York, NY: Square Fish, 2006.

Surmelis, Angelo. *The Dangerous Art of Blending In*. New York, NY: Balzer + Bray, 2018.

Zoboi, Ibi. *American Street*. New York, NY: Balzer + Bray, 2018.

Websites

Meet Young Immigrants
teacher.scholastic.com/activities/immigration/young_immigrants
This website, maintained by Scholastic, helps website visitors make an emotional connection with young immigrants.

National Immigration Forum
www.immigrationforum.org
This website features details on legislation, articles, and opinions favoring less restriction in immigration.

Teaching Tolerance
www.tolerance.org
This organization works to dispel myths surrounding racism, including those connected with immigration.

US Census Bureau
www.census.gov
Find detailed statistical demographic and population information on the US population dating back to the first census ever taken in 1790. Information about the foreign-born population and immigration history can also be found here.

US Customs and Border Protection
www.cbp.gov
This is the official website for CBP, which handles the task of protecting America's borders. Learn about CBP's job in great detail, as well as what life is like for a border patrol agent.

Organizations

American Immigration Council
1331 G Street NW, Suite 200
Washington, DC 20005
www.americanimmigrationcouncil.org
twitter.com/immcouncil
The American Immigration Council is a nonprofit, nonpartisan
organization committed to sensible and humane immigration
policies, as well as challenging myths and misconceptions
about immigrants.

The Brookings Institution
1775 Massachusetts Avenue NW
Washington, DC 20036
www.brookings.edu
twitter.com/BrookingsInst
www.youtube.com/user/BrookingsInstitution
The Brookings Institution is a private, nonprofit organization
devoted to independent research and innovative policy solutions.

National Association of Counsel for Children (NACC)
1600 Downing Street, Suite 410
Denver, CO 80218
www.naccchildlaw.org
twitter.com/NACCchildlaw
This organization gives legal aid to children and families.
Immigrant children who need legal help can contact the
NACC for advice.

Pew Research Center
1615 L Street NW, Suite 800
Washington, DC 20036
www.pewresearch.org
twitter.com/pewresearch
www.youtube.com/user/PewResearchCenter/featured
This nonpartisan organization provides information on the issues, attitudes, and trends shaping America and the world, including immigration issues. It does so by conducting public opinion polling and social science research, reporting news, analyzing news coverage, and holding forums and briefings. It does not take positions on policy issues.

Refugee and Immigrant Center for Education and Legal Services (RAICES)
1305 N Flores Street
San Antonio, TX 78212
www.raicestexas.org
www.instagram.com/raicestexas
twitter.com/raicestexas
www.youtube.com/raicestexas
RAICES is a nonprofit organization that provides free legal and social services to low-income immigrants.

INDEX

R

S

T

U

V

W

X

PHOTO CREDITS

Cover Kevin Sullivan/Orange County Register via Getty Images; p. 4 TZIDO SUN/Shutterstock.com; pp. 6-7 Joseph Sohm/Shutterstock.com; p. 10 Robert Alexander/Archive Photos/Getty Images; p. 13 Everett Historical/Shutterstock.com; p. 15 Illustrated London News/Hulton Archive/Getty Images; p. 18 FPG/Archive Photos/Getty Images; p. 20 © CORBIS/Corbis via Getty Images; p. 22 J R Eyerman/The LIFE Picture Collection via Getty Images; p. 24 Lyn Alweis/The Denver Post via Getty Images; p. 30 AshTproductions/Shutterstock.com; p. 32 donsimon/Shutterstock.com; p. 34 Joe Raedle/Getty Images News/Getty Images; p. 38 Orlando Sierra/AFP via Getty Images; p. 40 Marcelo A Salinas/Tribune News Service via Getty Images; p. 42 Ron de Vries/Construction Photography/Avalon/Getty Images; p. 47 fizkes/Shutterstock.com; p. 49 Olena Yakobchuk/Shutterstock.com; p. 52 TORWAISTUDIO/Shutterstock.com; p. 54 David Handschuh/NY Daily News Archive via Getty Images; p. 56 Jessica McGowan/Getty Images; p. 65 Stuart Monk/Shutterstock.com; p. 67 Allen.G/Shutterstock.com; p. 72 Ryan Rodrick Beiler/Shutterstock.com; p. 74 Rebekah Zemansky/Shutterstock.com; p. 77 Konrad Fiedler/AFP via Getty Images; p. 81 John Moore/Getty Images News/Getty Images; p. 82 Angela Weiss/AFP via Getty Images; p. 85 Noah Berger/AFP via Getty Images; p. 89 David McNew/Getty Images.

ABOUT THE AUTHOR

Meghan Green has edited a number of books for young people on the topics of social justice and self-esteem. She also sometimes gives talks at local schools on these topics. She is a social worker who specializes in working with developmentally disabled individuals. She lives in Pennsylvania with her husband, Kris.